To Ollie
for Christmas 2009
love from
        Grandpa and Granny

The Bumper Book
of Nature

The Bumper Book of Nature

Stephen Moss

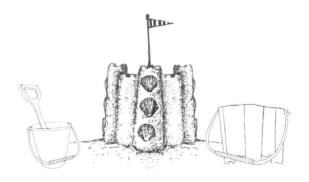

◨ SQUARE PEG

LONDON

For David and Martine Osorio,
for allowing us to be free-range children
instead of cotton-wool kids.

Contents

All Year Round

Summer

Naughty stuff 161

Things to do with flowers 164

Beside the seaside 176

Spring

Winter

Autumn

A note to parents *

(* and grandparents, godparents, aunts and uncles, big brothers and sisters, friends of the family, teachers, and anyone else who wants to get our children back in touch with nature ...)

When you think back to your own childhood, what do you remember? Did you climb trees, build dens, and fish for tiddlers? Of course you did – that's how we entertained ourselves in the days before computer games, mobile phones and a TV in every child's bedroom.

We didn't have the gadgets, the opportunities, or the sheer variety of ways today's children can spend their spare time. So to stave off boredom, we begged our parents to let us go and play outside. Ball games in the street were just the start – soon we were scrambling over the fence and into the woods, exploring nature for ourselves. Later on, in the summer holidays, we were sent out with our mum's words ringing in our ears – 'take care – and be back home for tea!'

OK, so I'm making our childhoods sound like something out of an Enid Blyton story. It wasn't always like that, of course. Sometimes we hurt ourselves – falling out of trees or grazing our knees. Sometimes we came home soaked through after being caught in the rain, and got a good telling off from Mum and Dad.

But all this time we were learning about nature: seeing tadpoles turn into frogs, making daisy chains, or simply watching the birds we came across in our wanderings. And by climbing trees and building dens we also learned about taking risks, working together as a team, and ultimately about our own limits.

So tell me, honestly: are today's children more happy and fulfilled than we were? Of course they aren't. In the past couple of decades, we have raised generations of children who are scared to walk in the park on their own, who scream when they encounter a spider or a moth, and who know more about the characters in TV soaps than they do about bluebells and bumblebees.

The consequences of this are very worrying. If we're not

careful, when these children grow up they will have no interest in, or passion for, the natural world — and if you don't care about something, what incentive is there to protect it?

So what can we do to get our children back in touch with nature? Well for a start I hope you, and any children you know, will use this book to get out and experience the wonders of the natural world for yourselves. This isn't hard — there are many things you can do in any back garden, or your local park. There are things you can do as a family, or your children can do on their own or with their friends. And there are organised activities, such as a dawn chorus walk, which are best enjoyed in the company of a knowledgeable expert.

I've arranged the activities into seasons, along with a substantial section of things you can do all year round. I've tried to be as specific as possible — if you already know how to climb a tree then you can skip the directions, but if it's the first time your children have done it, there are step-by-step instructions on the best way to do so.

To help you identify the animals and plants you see, I've included identification guides to common species, beautifully illustrated by some of Britain's finest wildlife artists. And there are poems, fascinating facts and snippets of folklore to keep you and your children entertained.

At the end of the book there are contact details of organisations, website addresses and a selection of books to help you extend your and your children's knowledge of Britain's wonderful natural heritage.

So please don't put *The Bumper Book of Nature* away on a bookshelf and let it gather dust. This is a book to be used, taken outdoors, to get muddy fingerprints on its pages. It is, I hope, a book for life — something you can enjoy with your children as they grow up, and which they may perhaps even use one day to introduce their own children to wildlife.

I am a very lucky man. As a child, I learned to explore the world around my home. I walked under blue suburban skies, built dens in the scrubby wood behind our house, played around the local gravel pits — and because of all this I developed a love of nature. In later life, I became one of those very fortunate people whose lifetime's passion is also their job, as the producer of wildlife television programmes such as *Springwatch*. I owe all this to one simple thing: that when I was growing up I was given the freedom that so many parents now deny their own children.

So now I want you to close your eyes, and imagine a world where you send your child out into the natural world as a matter of course, rather than a special event. And instead of pre-programming their every move, and organising their every moment, you give them one, simple instruction: 'Enjoy yourself – and be back home for tea …'

A note to children

If someone has given you this book, they must know that you are interested in nature — in birds and bees, foxes and frogs, blue-bells and butterflies, and all the other wonderful wild creatures out there.

But when was the last time you went outside and discovered nature for yourself — on your own or with your friends? Never? Maybe your parents are worried that you'll hurt yourself, or get dirty. Maybe you don't know where to go, or what to do, or how to tell what bird or flower you are looking at.

That's where *The Bumper Book of Nature* comes in. This book is packed full of exciting things to do — on your own, with friends, or with grown-ups. You can build a den, catch tadpoles, or play conkers. You can do something simple like lie down in the long grass and look up at the sky, or a bit trickier like keeping cater-pillars and watching them turn into butterflies. You can do these things in your garden, down at the local park, on a walk in the woods, or by the seaside; and in spring, summer, autumn and winter. Whatever the time of year, and whatever the weather, there's always something to see and do in the wild world!

To help you know what you are looking at, there are pictures of common animals and birds, plants and insects — so if you find a strange butterfly in your garden, or see an unusual bird on the park pond, you can find out what it's called. And at the end of the book there's loads of useful information — websites, books and organisations you can join to help you make the most of your interest in nature.

So I hope you won't just put this book away on your bedroom shelf and forget about it. This is a book you need to use, to take outdoors — even to get dirty! Make sure you ask a grown-up before you do any of the activities here; and if they want to come with you that's fine. But as you get older and more confident, ask them if you can go out with your friends and enjoy the natural world on your own.

And if, like me, you fall in love with nature, I can promise you that you'll never be bored again — because there's always something to see, to do and to enjoy.

Have fun!

All Year Round

The great thing about the natural world is that it never stops. Whatever the time of year, something interesting is going on — you just need to go out and discover it.

The rest of this book is arranged season by season, as there are many things that you can only do at a particular time of year — listen to the dawn chorus, watch dragonflies, play conkers or build a snowman.

But there are also quite a few things that you can do more or less any time of year, such as building a den, making a nature table and climbing a tree. You can play Poohsticks or go for a walk in a churchyard; skim stones or feed your garden birds; look for mammal tracks or start keeping a nature diary — or all of these things.

So there's no excuse — whatever the time of year, the natural world is out there just waiting for you to explore it!

Build a den

When I was growing up, one of my favourite pastimes was making a den in the woods at the back of our house. I say woods, but this was really just a narrow strip of elm trees and scrub between the bottom of our garden and the back lane. But to us it was 'the forest', and we spent many a happy hour creating cosy hideaways out of bits of wood and old rugs we found in the garage. A few years later, the elms were all chopped down because of Dutch elm disease, and our adventure playground vanished for ever.

Do you remember, when you were very young, pulling all the cushions off the chairs and sofas and piling them up to make yourself a little hideaway, where no one could find you?

It's even better to build a den outdoors — using fallen branches, bits of wood and old carpet to make a secret place all of your own. Your den can be as sophisticated or as simple as you want, but creating a good den that will withstand the gales and storms involves planning, construction and teamwork. Join forces with your friends or brothers and sisters and make it a project that you can all enjoy — a much better way to spend a weekend or holidays than sitting in front of a TV or computer!

Here are some tips on how to make a really good den

* You can make a den out of almost anything — natural or man-made — just as long as you can make walls and a roof, creating an enclosed space where you can hide away from the outside world.
* Keep it simple: larger bits of wood — either planks or fallen branches — will help you build a structure which you can cover with a blanket or rug to create a roof.
* Think about what you're trying to do: maybe draw a quick sketch on a bit of paper to show your friends.
* Listen to other people's advice — they may be able to improve on your design.
* Once you've got everything you need to build your den, start making the walls from the bottom up — use large branches or bits of wood to create the frame.
* When you've got the basic structure, cover it with a piece of material, such as an old sheet, blanket, rug or offcut of carpet — but *not* the best rug from the sitting room! If the material you use is waterproof so much the better — it will help to keep the inside of the den snug and dry.
* Then cover your den with smaller and lighter leafy branches to create a camouflage canopy — but don't forget to leave a gap large enough for a door!
* Bring another piece of material, or old duvet, to lay on the floor of the den to make it really comfortable.
* Once it's complete, stand back and admire your creation — your den is ready to be occupied.

* Bring along some food and drink and have an indoor picnic — outdoors.
* And once you're inside your den, sit quietly and see what's going on outside — a den can make an excellent hide for nature-watching.

And a few more tips

* A really quick and easy way to make a den is to hang a length of washing line between two tree trunks or branches, tied fast at either end, and then just drape an old sheet or blanket over the top. Secure the edges of the blanket with heavy stones or bits of wood, and hey presto! An instant den.
* For very young children, simply hang a duvet or rug over the backs of garden chairs and put a rug inside for them to sit on.

Make a nature table

Back in the 1950s, 60s and 70s every primary school had a nature table, where children could bring in items they had found at the weekends, or discovered on nature walks with their classmates.

Nature tables are the ideal way to mark the passing of the seasons — and to get to know about the incredible variety of natural objects you can collect.

Misguided fears about children coming to some sort of harm have more or less brought an end to this wonderful way of learning about the natural world. But there's no law against nature tables, and with a bit of common sense any potential hazards can be identified and removed. So why not start one yourself — at home or at school?

Things you can collect for your nature table

* Anything that falls off a tree: pine cones, dried leaves, acorns, prickly conkers in their cases, nuts and seeds, berries, fruit, whole twigs or small branches that have blown off in the wind.

* Pieces of tree bark you find on the ground.

* Dry thistle heads, seed pods, grasses, reeds and bulrushes, little clumps of moss or lichens.

* Flowers, which you can either keep in a jam jar full of water or press to preserve them. (See pages 164–6)

* Inanimate objects: stones, pebbles and rocks – look out for unusual shapes or colours. If you look in the right place some of them may even contain fossils.

* Birds' feathers – from pigeons, gulls, crows, birds of prey and smaller birds. Look out for real gems, like the gorgeous blue wing feather of the jay.

* Shells: either from the beach, or if you don't get to visit the seaside, from the snails and other creatures in your garden.

* Dead stuff – such as beetles (whose hard casing means they last a long time), spiders, or delicate skulls of birds.

* Old birds' nests (the nests are old, not the birds).

* Mushrooms and toadstools – just as long as you use rubber gloves and wash your hands carefully after you handle them.

You can also put out identification guides to help you identify what you find. (See back of book for details.)

Tip

To make your nature table even more exciting, add a glass tank where you can keep creatures you've collected, such as frogspawn (which will turn into tadpoles, then into frogs), or caterpillars (which will turn into pupae, then into butterflies), as well as minibeasts such as spiders, woodlice and snails.

Climb a tree

When was the last time you climbed a really good tree? Maybe you've been told not to climb trees because you might fall and hurt yourself. But what sort of a life is it if you never learn to take risks?

Actually, I'm a bit wary of climbing trees myself – but when I do have a go, I'm really glad I did. That's because tree climbing is a great way to learn the limits of your sense of adventure. It doesn't matter if you don't get all the way to the top – what's important is that you try your best, and perhaps get a little bit further each time.

How to identify …
large mammals

Britain's larger mammals include some of our commonest and
most familiar animals, as well as some of the rarest and most
difficult to see. In the first group are the rabbit, fox and badger;
while even the keenest mammal enthusiasts struggle to see pole-
cats, pine martens and the elusive Scottish wild cat.

After suffering at the hands of hunting and pollution, some
creatures, such as the otter, are making a comeback. Meanwhile,
one of our favourite mammals, the red squirrel, continues to
decline as a result of competition with the greys introduced from
North America.

As well as land-based mammals, don't forget the two species of
seal, both of which can be easily seen at special sites around our
coasts. Land-based mammals (e.g. deer) live excusively on land;
the term 'resident mammals' includes all land mammals and
coastal marine mammals which breed on land (e.g. seals), but
not whales.

How to identify ...
large mammals

Rabbit

The classic bunny of children's stories such as *Watership Down* is not a native British species at all, but was brought here by the Norman invaders for food. It is found all over lowland Britain — living together in networks of tunnels known as warrens. Best time to see them is to visit a warren in late afternoon on a warm summer's day when the youngsters are out playing.

Polecat

The ancestor of the domestic ferret, and very similar in appearance: with a dark body and paler belly, and a distinctive masked face pattern. Nocturnal, and very hard to see.

Stoat

The stoat is a lean, mean, killing machine — pound for pound our most voracious predator, and able to kill a rabbit many times its own weight. Larger and bulkier than the weasel, with a black tip to its tail. In hilly regions turns white in winter — known as 'ermine'.

Brown Hare

Larger than the rabbit, with much longer, black-tipped ears, and very long hind legs, enabling it to run very fast. Unlike rabbits, hares do not use burrows — instead, when frightened, they'll crouch low into a hollow known as a 'form'. In spring, watch out for 'mad March hares' boxing — as females test out rival males for strength and persistence.

Mountain Hare

This slightly smaller relative of the brown hare is found in hilly and mountainous regions of Scotland, Ireland and the Peak District in England. In winter, the mountain hare is one of the few British mammals whose coat turns white, as camouflage against predators in its snowy home.

Otter

This beautiful creature has made a comeback in recent years and is now found in rivers and waterways throughout Britain — even in some cities. Large, sleek and equally suited to water or land. Otters are often nocturnal, but on Scottish coasts may be seen at any time of day, as their lifestyle is governed by the tides.

North American Mink

An introduced mammal which has wreaked havoc on our native animals such as the water vole. Smaller and darker than the otter, and also found in rivers, streams and other waterways. May now be declining as a result of the otter's comeback.

Weasel

Smaller than the closely related stoat — a long, slender creature usually seen briefly as it dashes across a road or path before disappearing into a grassy verge. If you get good views, look out for the tail, which lacks the stoat's black tip.

Red Squirrel

Britain's native squirrel has suffered major declines in numbers and range during the last century, and is now only found in Scotland, Ireland, parts of northern England and Wales, and a few outposts in southern England. Unmistakable, with reddish-brown fur and those tufty ears.

Grey Squirrel

Not the most popular British mammal, and not really British at all, but introduced from North America over a hundred years ago. Nevertheless, grey squirrels can provide hours of entertainment as they try to raid your bird feeders. Common throughout most of the country.

Pine Marten

This beautiful creature can be found in parts of Scotland and Ireland, and although very shy has been known to come to bird tables to feed. Chestnut brown above and buff below, with a long body and tail.

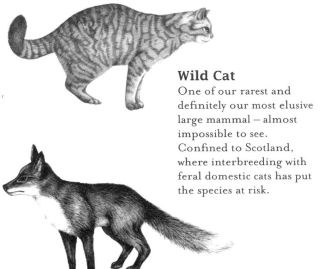

Wild Cat

One of our rarest and definitely our most elusive large mammal – almost impossible to see. Confined to Scotland, where interbreeding with feral domestic cats has put the species at risk.

Badger

The legendary 'brock' is one of our easiest mammals to recognise — with its dark grey body, stocky appearance and black-and-white face pattern. Common and widespread, but because of its nocturnal habits not always easy to see.

Fox

This originally rural, shy animal is nowadays most likely to be seen in our towns and cities. Here it is transformed into a cocky, streetwise creature, roaming the urban jungle and scavenging for food from dustbins. Our only wild dog, easily recognised by its reddish-brown coat.

Wild Boar

This ancient forest dweller went extinct in Britain centuries ago, but has made a comeback after escaping from farms in parts of southern Britain. Most likely to be seen crossing a road in a forested area.

Common Seal

Smaller and more friendly-looking than the grey seal – and actually less common – with a doglike facial expression. Comes in variety of colours, and found around our coasts, especially in Scotland.

Grey Seal

Our largest resident mammal, and the larger and commoner of our two species of seal. Told apart from common seal by more haughty appearance with massive nose. Found around our coasts, especially in the north and west.

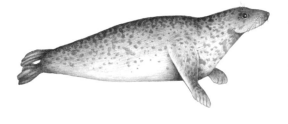

* Late autumn and winter are the best time for climbing: once the leaves have fallen off it's easier to see what you're doing. But you can climb trees at any time of the year.
* Old jeans and a long-sleeved top are better than shorts and T-shirts, as they stop you grazing your knees and elbows. Wear shoes with a really strong grip — trainers rather than sandals, plimsolls or wellies.
* Choose the right sort of tree: large, old trees are best as they have stronger branches, and fewer twigs to get in the way. Beech trees are great: the bark is good for gripping, and their branches stick out at right angles from the trunk. Oak trees are also good.
* Dead trees are tempting to climb, but remember that their branches are more likely to snap.
* Take a few minutes to work out your route before you start climbing. Make sure your feet support the weight of your body, and that you always have at least one hand firmly gripping a branch.
* If you're not sure a branch is thick enough to take your weight, test it first by pulling hard with your free hand. And don't rush — that's the sure way to fall.
* Once you find a comfortable spot halfway up a tree, sit down on a branch and have a good look around. You're seeing the world in a different way from usual — from above. Spend a few minutes quietly looking and listening, and you'll be amazed at what you discover.
* Climbing down is actually more risky than going up: so once again take your time, and make sure your feet and hands are in the right place each time you move, and that you have a firm footing as you descend.

The tree you are climbing could be as much as five hundred years old — which means it was growing at the time Queen Elizabeth I was on the throne. And the largest tree in Britain, the thousand-year-old Bowthorpe Oak in Lincolnshire, is so big it is possible to hold a tea party inside its hollow trunk.

Hang upside down from the branch of a tree

Next time you're walking through a wood, find a large, mature tree with a thick, horizontal branch sticking out from the trunk, a couple of metres above the ground. Climb up to the branch; then carefully hook your legs over the branch and hang upside down from it. It's a whole new way of seeing a familiar world.

Make a rope swing from a tree

One of the most enjoyable things to do in your garden or a local wood is to make a rope swing. Because it can move in any direction, instead of just backwards and forwards like swings in a playground, a rope swing is much more fun than a conventional one.

You will need

* A length of high-quality rope about three centimetres thick, and long enough to reach from your chosen branch to the ground plus another metre or so to be safe.
* A round disc of wood — perhaps an old chopping board, or a cross-section through a treetrunk, large enough to sit on and thick enough to support your weight (at least three centimetres, preferably thicker).
* Some sandpaper and a sanding block if you need to smooth the edges of the wood.
* An electric drill.
* A ladder.

Find your tree

Choose a big, solid tree, with a strong branch from which to hang your swing. Look for a mature, healthy tree such as an oak or beech, with thick, horizontal branches at least thirty centimetres across. Choose a branch growing between three and four metres above the ground. Check beneath where you plan to hang your swing to make sure the ground is reasonably level, and that there aren't any sharp objects such as tree stumps or big rocks, which might hurt you if you fall off.

Now, make your swing

* Using the electric drill, make a hole in the centre of the piece of wood, wide enough to thread your rope through.
* Place the ladder securely against the branch, and tie one end of the rope around the branch — ideally using a bowline knot which will hold it secure. The bowline is one of the easiest and most effective of knots.
* Decide how high you want the seat (about one metre off the ground is best).
* Getting someone else to hold the seat in position, thread the rope through the hole in the centre and tie a thick knot beneath the seat to hold the rope in place — you may want to tie at least three knots here.
* Give a firm tug before you start using it to make sure everything is secure.
* Then enjoy having a swing!

Tell the age of a tree

It's quite hard to tell the exact age of most living creatures. Once a baby bird has fledged and moulted into its adult plumage it will

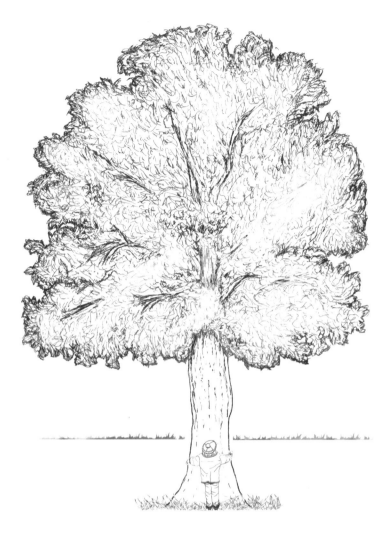

look the same whether it's two or twenty years old. The same goes for other animals.

But one group of living things has made it a lot easier for us, at least once they've died. If you look at the cross section of a tree trunk, you can see a series of rings, each inside another, from the centre to the edge. Each ring represents one year of that tree's life; so by counting them you can work out how old that particular tree is.

But there's much more to tree rings than simply using them to work out the age of a tree. Scientists can measure the distance between each ring to work out whether or not a particular year was a good or bad one — a hot, dry summer, for example, will limit growth that year, producing a narrow gap between rings;

while a warm, wet summer will allow the tree to grow faster, producing a wide one. This is known as 'dendrochronology', and is used by scientists to measure climate change.

To count tree rings for yourself, you first need to find a dead tree, preferably one that has been felled so that either the trunk or its stump remains. Rings are counted from the centre outwards — the ones nearest the centre are the oldest, and those closest to the bark are the most recent.

Most large felled trees will be between fifty and hundred years old, but some large ones — especially oaks — may be several hundred years of age.

But, can you tell the age of a living tree, *without* cutting it down?

Yes you can — not quite as accurately as with a dead tree, but still close enough.

Using a tape measure, measure the girth (the distance around the tree) about one and a half metres above the ground. Then apply one of the following rules:

* If the tree is surrounded by lots of other trees (so has had to compete with them for the sunlight needed to grow), every 12mm of girth equals a year's growth.
* If the tree is standing on its own, with plenty of access to sunlight, then every 25mm of girth equals a year's growth.

So a tree in a forest measuring about two metres around is over one hundred and fifty years old; while the same sized tree standing alone is only about eighty years old. A word of warning, though: some species grow more quickly than others — for instance, a pine tree or sycamore will usually be older than an oak of similar girth.

The oldest tree in Europe is believed to be the famous Fortingall Yew, in Perthshire, Scotland — reliably estimated to be about 5,000 years of age. This means it was already growing when Stonehenge and the Great Pyramids of Giza were built, and into middle age when the Romans invaded Britain.

Make a bark rubbing

This is a good way to appreciate the patterns made by the bark of a tree, and can also be used to identify different kinds of tree — though it's often easier to look at the leaves and the general shape of the tree to tell what it is.

What to do

* Place a piece of plain white paper up against the bark of a large, mature tree.
* Using a pencil or crayon, rub firmly and evenly across the surface of the paper so that the pattern of the bark is revealed.
* Once you've made several different bark rubbings, lay them side by side so you can compare the different patterns made by different kinds of tree.

bark rubbing of London plane

Tip

By using a large roll of plain white lining paper (which you can get from your local DIY store), you can make a continuous bark rubbing using different coloured crayons, which you can then use to wrap birthday and Christmas presents.

Listen to a tree

Believe it or not, you can actually listen to a tree – an experience which really does give you a new way of understanding the living world.

All you need is a recording and listening device known as a contact microphone – the kind that musicians use to record the sound of individual instruments such as a guitar or piano. They are not very expensive (£10–£50) and can be bought from any specialist electrical retailer. You may also want a pair of head-phones to make it easier to listen.

You can either connect it to an amplifier and speaker so you can listen to what is being picked up at the time; or plug it into any recording device such as a minidisc or even a video camcord-er, and record the sound to listen to later.

To listen to a tree, carefully place your contact microphone inside a hollow trunk, against its surface; plug it in, and wait. You should hear all sorts of strange sounds – most of which are made by tiny grubs nibbling away at the wood. Remember that you need to make sure the microphone is in direct contact with the tree or it won't work.

Tip

You can also use your contact microphone to listen to and record other natural sounds, such as an ants' nest or even the in-side of a compost heap. Again, make sure it is pressed up against the surface of whatever you are listening to.

Look for owl pellets

David, the father of my old school friend Daniel, recalls that when he was growing up during the 1940s and 50s he and his

How to identify ...
birds of prey in flight

We don't get many good news stories with our wildlife, but here's one. As a child, I hardly ever saw a bird of prey apart from the odd kestrel. Nowadays, I can see six different species in a day within a few miles of my home.

That's because in the past few years the number of birds of prey in Britain has rocketed, mainly because they are no longer shot and trapped as much as they used to be. But our various falcons, hawks, harriers, kites and eagles are not always easy to identify — you rely more on shape, behaviour and what birders call 'jizz' than on colour and pattern.

With practice, though, you should be able to put a name to most birds of prey that you see. But remember that female and male birds of the same species often appear quite different — not just in colour, but also because the female is generally a fair bit larger than her mate.

How to identify ...
birds of prey in flight

Sparrowhawk
Similar in size to a kestrel (though females are noticeably larger), but a very different shape: short, rounded wings and a long tail. Sparrowhawks are often seen flying high in sunny weather – alternating flaps with long glides; or shooting low through the garden in pursuit of its songbird prey.

Kestrel
Once our commonest bird of prey, it is now being challenged and perhaps even overtaken by the buzzard. The kestrel is the 'hawk' that hovers along roadside verges – hanging stock-still in the air on long, narrow wings, before plummeting down to catch some unsuspecting vole.

Buzzard
Our largest common bird of prey – with a short, rounded tail and long wings with 'fingers' at the ends. On sunny days soars in the sky, using thermal air currents to gain height. In Scotland, it is often mistaken for the much rarer (and larger) golden eagle.

Hobby
A summer visitor to our shores, arriving in May and leaving in September. Smaller, slimmer and darker than the kestrel, and usually found over water in southern Britain. Often hunts in groups, chasing and catching dragonflies and swallows.

Peregrine
Our largest falcon and the fastest creature on the planet. Large and stocky, dark above and pale below, with powerful wingbeats. Now found in many cities as well as the countryside and coast.

Harriers

Three species of harrier are found in Britain: marsh, hen and Montagu's. All are slender, long-winged birds which glide low on V-shaped wings. Marsh breeds mainly in eastern Britain, preferring reed beds; hen is a bird of the northern moors, though can be seen on coastal marshes in winter; while Montagu's is extremely rare, found only at a few sites in southern and eastern England.

Red Kite

Once incredibly rare, this elegant bird has now been reintroduced into various parts of the country, including the Chilterns, the East Midlands, and Black Isle and the Borders in Scotland. One of the best places to see them is from the M40 motorway south-east of Oxford. Unmistakable when seen: no other bird has the kite's combination of long, narrow wings, forked tail and reddish plumage.

Osprey

Also known as the 'fish hawk', the osprey went extinct in Britain but returned naturally. Now breeds all over Scotland, generally by lochs, with a few pairs in Wales and England. Buzzard-sized, with very pale underparts and a dark mask through the eye. Sometimes seen on migration in the spring and autumn.

Golden Eagle

Apart from the odd bird in the English Lake District, this magnificent mountain dweller is confined to the Scottish Highlands. Huge, with long, broad wings; dark brown, with a golden patch on the side of the neck. Beware confusion with buzzards, which can look big, especially at close range.

White-tailed or Sea Eagle

Sea eagles were persecuted to extinction in Britain in the early twentieth century, but have now been reintroduced to both the west and east coasts of Scotland, with releases in southern England planned. Huge — even larger than the golden eagle — with massive wings, a pale head and that distinctive white tail.

friends would regularly dissect owl pellets to reveal their contents. Afterwards, the challenge was to put the various tiny body parts together to create the skeleton of the owl's prey – rather like assembling an Airfix model, but without the instructions.

Owl pellets are incredible things. They look like small bundles of grey fluff – until you start pulling them apart to reveal their contents. For inside the furry outer layer you will find all sorts of grisly objects: the bones and skull of whatever was the owl's most recent meal. They are produced because the owl swallows its prey whole, but is unable digest the fur and bones, so has to cough them up in a pellet.

You will need

* A bucket of warm water.
* A pair of tweezers.
* A magnifying glass.

What to do

* The best place to look for owl pellets is on the ground beneath where the owl roosts by day. Tawny owls usually roost in a large, mature tree, while barn owls prefer to stay inside barns or other farm buildings as well as churches.
* Scan the ground, searching for grey, furry-looking oval objects a few centimetres long.

* Once you've found a pellet, the best way to open it up without damaging the contents is to soak it in a bucket of warm water for an hour or so.
* Then, using the tweezers, gently tease it apart and pick out the clean skulls, vertebrae and other bones.

The vast majority of owls' prey is small rodents, such as wood mice, field and bank voles. With practice (and using a magnifying glass), you will soon be able to tell which body part, and sometimes which species, you are looking at. Individual bones such as vertebrae, the femur and jawbone are fairly easy to identify, looking remarkably like miniature versions of our own.

There are five different kinds of owl regularly found in Britain: the tawny, barn, little, long-eared and short-eared. Two other species are also sometimes seen here: snowy owls used to nest on the Shetland island of Fetlar, while a few pairs of eagle owls (the world's largest owl) have just started to breed in parts of northern England.

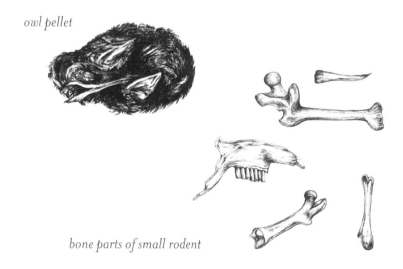

owl pellet

bone parts of small rodent

Look for mammal tracks and signs

Of the sixty or so different kinds of wild mammal found in Britain, almost a quarter are bats, while another twenty or so are classified as 'small mammals' — rats, mice, shrews and voles.

Many of these creatures are nocturnal, while others are so good at hiding from predators that you hardly ever see them. So the only wild mammals you are likely to come across are deer, rabbits, foxes and grey squirrels.

The good news is that many mammals do leave signs of where they've been — if only we knew how to read them. So why not turn mammal detective, and see what you can discover?

What to look for

* Skulls and bones: when an animal dies, its body soon disappears, either because it decomposes or is eaten by another animal. But the skeleton — including the skull — is usually left untouched. With practice, you can pick out the telltale bleached white of bones. But remember, domestic animals like sheep and cows die too, so you have to eliminate these first before you can be sure that your trophy comes from a truly wild animal.

* Antlers: in deer parks and other deer hotspots look out for shed antlers — especially towards the end of the autumn, when the fighting males lose their antlers to conserve energy for the winter ahead. Antlers are amazing — one of the fastest growing things in the natural world.

* Droppings: not for the squeamish, droppings are actually one of the very best ways to detect the presence of a particular creature. We hardly ever see otters, as they are mainly nocturnal, but it is quite easy to find their droppings (known as 'spraints') — they are dark and tar-like, with a distinctive fishy smell.

* Tracks: footprints — left behind in soft mud or sand — are another good way to detect if a particular creature lives in your neighbourhood.

front   *hind*

wood mouse

cat

* Hair: it's worth checking barbed-wire fences for bits of hair left behind as an animal squeezes through — for example, badgers often leave tufts of hair behind.
* Other signs: walk along a beach (especially just after autumn or winter gales) and you might come across the carcass of a marine mammal such as a dolphin or whale. Seeing the remains of these huge creatures at such close quarters always brings a mixture of wonder and sadness.

dog

Make a plaster cast of an animal track

One way to preserve what you find is to make a plaster cast of footprints or tracks made by passing mammals or birds. The best places to look for tracks are in soft mud around the edge of a pond, or in fresh snow.

front *fox*

front *hind* *rabbit*

front *hind* *squirrel*

front *hind* *hedgehog*

deer

front *hind* *weasel*

otter

You will need

* A soft brush (a large paintbrush is ideal).
* A syringe or pipette.
* Some small strips of wood or flexible plastic strip (to make a frame around the track and hold the plaster in).
* Plaster of Paris (bought from a modelling shop or DIY store).
* A bucket or plastic container to mix the plaster.
* A stick or an old wooden spoon for mixing.

Making your plaster of Paris

* Add the plaster slowly to the water in the ratio of two parts plaster to five parts water.
* Mix it slowly using a stick or old wooden spoon – NEVER mix using your hands as plaster of Paris can cause severe burns when in contact with skin.
* When the plaster is roughly the consistency of whipped cream it is ready to use.

How to make your plaster cast

* With the brush, carefully remove any bits of dirt or stones in and around the footprint.
* Then, using your syringe or pipette, suck up any water in the footprint – but be careful not to damage the outline of the print.
* Press your strips of wood or flexible plastic strip lightly into the earth, mud or snow to make a frame around the footprint.
* Gently pour the plaster into the track until it reaches the same level as the surface of the mud or snow.
* Wait until the plaster is partly set (an hour or two), then remove the outer frame as carefully as you can.
* Wrap up the cast in some newspaper or bubble wrap, take it home, and leave it in a cool, dry place to set properly (which usually takes a week or so).

mallard duck

Once your cast is ready, you can paint it using poster paints and put it in a display with other casts – don't forget to label each one so you know which animal made it.

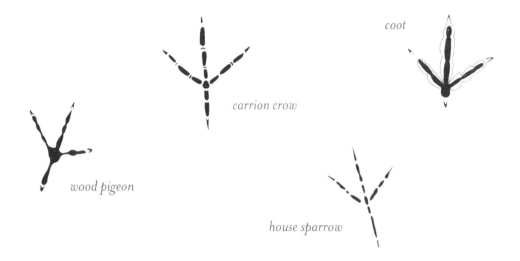

coot

carrion crow

wood pigeon

house sparrow

Grow mustard and cress

Growing mustard and cress on your kitchen windowsill is one of the best ways to watch how plants grow – the seeds sprout really quickly, and what's more, you get something to eat at the end of it!

You will need

* A plate, saucer or empty plastic strawberry punnet.
* Some paper towels.
* Mustard and cress seeds.

What to do

* Dampen about four or five pieces of folded kitchen paper with water and place the pieces on to a plate or saucer, or inside the bottom of an empty strawberry punnet.

* Sprinkle the seeds on top of the paper.
* Every day or so, sprinkle water on top to keep the seeds damp.
* Then watch them grow.

Once your mustard and cress is ready (after two or three weeks), cut it with scissors and serve sprinkled over salad or mixed with hard-boiled egg to make delicious egg-and-cress sandwiches.

Stand out in the rain

My grandmother firmly believed that getting caught in the rain was a sure-fire way to catch a cold — and in those days before central heating she was probably right. So to please grandmothers

everywhere, only do this when you're feeling fit as a fiddle, and have a warm, dry towel ready for when you come inside.

As the lyrics of an old song say, 'Remember — walking in the rain?'. But when was the last time you deliberately went out in the rain — without an umbrella — and got wet?

Yet feeling the rain run down your face is one of the best ways to really feel alive. It doesn't have to be for long — just time enough to appreciate the sensation of pure rainwater, and to remember that without this stuff, there wouldn't be any nature to enjoy.

Sit or stand still for an hour, just watching and listening

If you are someone who likes to be on the move when watching wildlife, seeing new things all the time, this can be really tough. But you'll be amazed how different the natural world appears when you experience it from a single place for a period of time. You can do this with or without binoculars — it's up to you. To be honest, I think it's better without, so you can really take in everything you see and hear. You can always have your binoculars handy in case you spot something really unusual.

It couldn't be simpler: just find a comfortable place, either sit or stand still for a whole hour, and see what turns up. Whether you're in your own garden, a city park, in the middle of a wood or on top of a mountain, I can guarantee you'll see or hear something different and new. I prefer doing this in a familiar place, as it brings a completely new perspective to your usual experience. Pay special attention to what each creature is doing, and ask yourself questions. Is that the same robin I saw a few minutes ago, or a different one? What is that squirrel doing? How many butterflies can I see at once? Anything and everything is worth looking at — and when the time is finally up, you'll never look at a familiar place in quite the same way again.

Do a 'blind walk'

We talk about 'wildlife-watching', but in fact a lot of the way we experience nature happens through other senses — especially hearing, smell and touch. So why not try an experiment that will help you appreciate these different senses a bit more?

Using a clean handkerchief or scarf, make a blindfold for yourself, making sure that you can't peek out the sides.

Then get someone you trust to guide you around a familiar place: your garden or the local park are ideal.

Start by standing still and listening. What can you hear? Depending where you are, you may have to ignore the sounds of traffic or aircraft. If you're doing this in spring or summer, can you hear the birds singing? In summer, if you get close to some flowers, you may also be able to hear the buzz of insects.

What about smell? Again, ask your companion to guide you towards some flowers, and take a deep, long sniff. Different flowers have very different scents.

Next, try touch. Ask your guide to hand you natural objects: a leaf, a bit of bark, or a flower. Can you tell what it is just by feeling it? Check out its shape: you may even be able to identify particular leaves, or familiar objects such as conkers, by touch alone.

If you feel a bit braver, get your guide to walk you around a larger area. Notice how the sounds and smells change depending on where you are. You should be able to tell whether you are in light or shade — for example, if you walk under a large tree or into a forest clearing.

When you feel you've had enough, swap over and get your guide to do the same as you. This time watch how they notice things without using their sight. Are they having the same experience as you or a different one?

And when you get home, write your impressions in your nature diary, making sure you record how you felt, and what was different about doing without a sense we take for granted — our sight.

Play Poohsticks

Fans of A. A. Milne's Winnie-the-Pooh books will already be familiar with this delightful game, which is easy to play and great fun. You can do it on any bridge over a stream or small river — just so long as the water flows underneath.

The rules are simple: each player finds a stick about a foot or so long; then you all drop your sticks, at the same time, on the upstream side of the bridge; and run over to the other side to see whose stick comes through first.

The game of Poohsticks first appeared in the book House at Pooh Corner, *published in 1928 — though children have been playing similar games for centuries. The annual World Poohsticks Championship is held in late March at Days Lock, Little Wittenham, in Oxfordshire.*

43

Climb the highest hill near where you live

Hillwalking is a very popular pastime in Britain. Some people take it to extremes, such as those whose aim is to climb every single peak over 3,000 feet (about 920 metres) in Britain. There are almost three hundred of these, and those in Scotland (the vast majority) are known as 'Munros' after the man who first made a list of them.

For less energetic climbers, a new category has been devised — known as 'Marilyns'. A Marilyn is any peak that is more than 500 feet (about 150 metres) higher than the surrounding countryside — meaning that although some of them aren't all that high, you do get fabulous views from them.

Most mountains — and therefore most Munros and Marilyns — are in Scotland and Wales. But if you live in the south or east, don't despair — there are plenty of hills here too. And while they might not be quite as high as Ben Nevis, or as scenic as Snowdonia, they are still great places for a day's walk.

Roll down a hill

Lie at the top of a dry, grassy slope (first making sure that there are no nasty things you might hit on the way down), and start rolling. If you want to stop, just stick your arms and legs out into a star shape.

Feed the birds in your garden

When I was a child, my grandmother would throw out a few scraps of suet, or crusts of stale bread, on to our back lawn — and the birds were suitably grateful. Later on, I would persuade my mother to buy 'Swoop' bird food, or one of those little red string bags full of peanuts, from the local pet shop. I could never have imagined that forty years later feeding birds would have turned into a huge industry, with well over one hundred different species having been recorded coming to bird feeders.

Two out of three of us regularly feed garden birds — anything from throwing out a few leftovers to creating a five-star service station complete with designer foods and feeders. By doing so, we get a lot of pleasure from what is one of the best, and easiest, ways to get close to nature.

The great thing about feeding birds is that you get instant results. More or less whatever food you put out, within minutes a bird will come and take advantage of a free meal. And this is true whether you live in the heart of the country or the middle of the city — birds are everywhere.

How to identify ...
garden birds

If you want to learn how to identify birds, then your garden is a great place to start. Put up a bird table and some feeders and you'll soon be able to take a good look at the birds that visit — and get to know the differences between them.

You probably already know more than you think. Most people can notice the difference between a song thrush and a blackbird, or tell a house sparrow apart from a starling. Robins are easy, and with practice, you'll soon be sorting out the various tits and finches that come to your feeders.

Use the illustrations here as a guide to get you started, but if you're not sure what a bird is, then check it out in a proper bird book to make sure. (See tips on choosing an identification guide at the back of this book.)

How to identify ...
garden birds

Collared Dove

Smaller and more delicate than Wood Pigeon. Mainly pinkish buff, with a black collar around the neck. Three-syllable call, sounds like 'U-ni-ted, u-ni-ted'!

Wood Pigeon

Large, plump pigeon with grey back, pinkish breast and obvious white ring around its neck. Five-syllable call, sounds like 'my toe is bleeding'!

Pied Wagtail

Delightful little black-and-white bird with a long tail, usually seen walking around on the lawn, driveway or pavement, picking up tiny insects with its long, pointed bill.

Wren

One of our smallest birds — and the commonest in Britain — but quite shy and retiring, so it's easy to miss. Look for a tiny brown bird with a short, cocked tail. And in spring, listen for the wren's loud, trilling song.

Dunnock

An unassuming little bird: robin-shaped but with markings similar to a sparrow — hence its old name of 'hedge sparrow'. Look for the long, pointed bill and greyish-mauve head and neck.

Great Spotted Woodpecker

Smart, starling-sized, black-and-white woodpecker with bright crimson patch under the tail, and with the male, on the back of the head. May come to bird feeders, but quite shy.

Robin

Adults unmistakable: brown above with orange-red breast and pale belly. Youngsters lack the red breast and are spotty, but have the same plump shape and beady eye as their parents.

Blackbird

Male easy to identify, with his all-black plumage, beady eye and bright custard-yellow bill. Females and youngsters are brown, but plain (not spotted like the thrushes).

Song Thrush

The classic thrush, with a spotty breast and chocolate-brown upperparts. The scarcer mistle thrush is much larger, paler and greyer, and has a less 'friendly' expression.

Jay
A shy relative of the magpie, with a stunning pink plumage, streaky crest, black bill, wings and tail, and a bright blue patch on its wings.

Blue Tit
A garden favourite: tiny, active and always looking for trouble! Blue head and back contrasts with white cheeks and yellow underneath. Loves seed and nut feeders and nest boxes.

Great Tit
Larger than blue tit, with no blue in the plumage at all. Look out for the black head contrasting with white cheeks, moss-green back, and yellow underparts with a thick black line running down the middle.

Starling
Often ignored, Starlings deserve a closer look. Their plumage shines with glossy greens and purples (especially in summer), while in winter they are covered in tiny white spots. Check out the base of the yellow bill: blue for a male, pink for a female – honestly!

Jackdaw
Our smallest crow, mainly black apart from a light grey patch on the back of its neck. Short, stubby bill. Sociable, and often seen in noisy flocks.

Magpie
The classic pantomime villain of the garden: this noisy, brash black-and-white bird is actually a real beauty, with subtle greens and purples in its plumage, which are easiest to see when the sun shines.

House Sparrow
Sociable, cheeky little bird, usually seen in a group. Males have a black bib, grey head, pale grey cheeks and brown back. Females are duller brown; plain beneath and streaky above.

Goldfinch
Beautiful little finch, with a crimson face patch, black-and-white head pattern, and black wings with a golden-yellow stripe which is even more obvious when they fly. Sharp beak for feeding on tiny seeds. Usually seen in flocks.

Greenfinch
Males easy to spot, with their moss-green plumage and yellow in the wing. Females and youngsters can be confused with sparrows, but always show some yellow or green colour in their feathers.

Chaffinch
The male is one of our handsomest birds: pink below, with a grey head and two bright white wing bars. Female looks a bit like a female sparrow, but has cleaner plumage and white wing bars.

But if you really want to make a difference to your local birds — and get the most out of feeding them — you need to make a bit more of an effort. Here are ten top tips for feeding garden birds.

* Choose good-quality food. That means high-energy seeds such as sunflower hearts rather than peanuts. Sunflower hearts have a much higher oil content, which means the birds don't have to feed for so long to get the same amount of energy. In the short winter days, choosing sunflower hearts over peanuts will save many birds' lives.
* Buy from a reputable supplier. Be careful who you buy your food from. Many garden centres and pet-food suppliers now stock good-quality food from leading bird-food companies; but others don't. If in doubt, get your food by mail order from one of the companies that advertise in birding and wildlife magazines, or from the RSPB.
* Once you start feeding — don't stop. It's easy to be enthusiastic at the start, but when the first batch of food runs out many people forget to order more, and the feeders run empty. That's the worst thing you can do, as your garden birds will have begun to depend on you for food — so keep those feeders filled.

* Feed birds all year round. We used to feed birds only during the winter months, when short days and harsh weather mean they need extra food. But breeding birds and their chicks need energy just as much, so it's best to feed all year round.

* Have a bird table as well as seed feeders. Bird tables allow species that can't cling to hanging feeders, such as doves, pigeons, blackbirds and thrushes, to enjoy the food on offer as well. You can put all sorts of different foods on a bird table — from cooked rice to raisins, and from leftover pastry to bits of fruit. Cooked bacon rind and grated cheese are also very popular.

* Clean your feeders regularly. Dirty feeders, with rotting food, can easily spread disease; so give them a regular clean with soap and water, and remember to throw away any food that isn't eaten after a day or two.

* Give birds live food. Birds like robins and blackbirds love mealworms, which you can buy through mail order. Put them out in the breeding season, when both the adults and chicks need extra energy.

* Just add water — with a bird bath. Birds don't just want food — they need a place to drink and wash themselves as well. Bird baths come in all shapes and sizes, from classic stone to modern plastic. Make sure that the sides of the bath are shallow enough for small birds to bathe safely, that you keep it topped up, and that you clean it at least once a week to prevent disease.

* Make your garden bird-friendly. Providing birds with a self-service restaurant is just the start — you can attract a far greater range of species to your garden by making it a five-star hotel as well. So don't forget nest boxes; and plant some native flowers, trees and shrubs which attract insects and provide a place where the birds can roost at night.

* Keep a record of the birds you see. Keeping a notebook or diary of the different birds in your garden — and noting down any interesting behaviour — is part of the fun. Looking back in years to come, you'll be amazed at the variety of birds you've seen, and be able to enjoy recalling memories of what they were doing.

49

And if you're really keen

Take part in a bird survey. Either the annual Big Garden Bird-watch run each January by the RSPB, or the year-round Garden BirdWatch survey run by the BTO – or why not both? Details of how to take part are at the back of this book. (See Winter.)

A blue tit, weighing between eight and twelve grams, needs to eat about forty per cent of its body weight every day, just to survive. That's equivalent to you or me eating about eighty roast dinners, one hundred and sixty bowls of cereal or almost five hundred Mars bars – every single day …

A recipe for a fatball for the birds

This may not win any awards for culinary excellence, but the birds really love it. And it's a lot cheaper than buying fatballs from the shop.

What you need

* A large saucepan.
* Some lard or suet.
* Nuts, seeds and raisins to add energy.
* A coconut shell, cut in two, and with the flesh scraped out.
* Some string.

What to do

* Before you start, drill a small hole in the top of the coconut shell and thread your string through, tying a knot to make it secure.
* Warm the fat in a large saucepan over a low heat, being careful not to let it get too hot.
* Mix in the seeds, nuts and raisins.

* As the fat starts to cool, pour the mixture into your half coconut shell until it reaches the top.
* Leave for an hour or two to harden – in the fridge if the weather is warm.
* Once it's hard enough, hang it up and wait for the birds to come.

Tip

If you can't get hold of a coconut, you can always use a large plastic or paper cup. Pierce a hole in the bottom of the cup, thread a piece of string through it and fill the cup to the brim with the fat mixture.

Keep a nature notebook and diary

Once you start noticing different wildlife all around you, you might want to keep a written diary of what you see. Over the years you'll find that your nature diaries form not just a record of your sightings, but also something you can look back over and remember wonderful days out in the countryside, or memorable encounters with wildlife. I used to write down sightings in notebooks but now find it easier to type my records straight into the computer. But it doesn't matter how you keep your records, just make sure you do it in the first place.

Tips

* Always write down the key facts:
  · Date (you can use a desk diary to make this easier)
  · Location – e.g. 'my garden', 'the New Forest', or if you want real detail, use the six-figure Ordnance Survey reference (e.g. SP 896423)

- Time of sighting/time spent in the field
- Who you were with
- Weather conditions: sunny, cloudy or wet? Approximate temperature, etc.
- Names of species you saw
- Any interesting or unusual behaviour
- Memorable moments

✳ It's a good idea to have two notebooks: a small, portable one to take out on walks, and a larger one to write up your sightings and experiences when you get home.

✳ A handy alternative to a field notebook is a small portable voice recorder — either an old-fashioned tape or newer digital version. They save your fingers getting cold, and enable you to watch a bird or animal at the same time as recording what it's doing — but make sure you carry a spare set of batteries.

✳ If you see something you can't identify, concentrate on getting the essentials down on paper or tape, such as what it looks like. This is especially important if it's a bird — they do tend to fly away before you've taken proper notes. When you get home you can look up the mystery creature in your field guide.

Remember your nature diary doesn't have to be a record of visits to exotic or far-flung locations — the most rewarding diary you keep is likely to be the one of sightings in your garden.

Go for a walk in a churchyard

When it comes to looking for wild animals and plants, it's easy to overlook one of the best places of all — and one that can be found in most villages, towns and cities in the country — a churchyard.

Because of their great age (many Christian churches are hundreds of years old, and were often built on even older sites of pagan worship), churchyards offer wildlife a real sanctuary.

From season to season, year to year and century to century,

churchyards provide an undisturbed place where all God's creatures can find a home. Few other places in Britain have remained more or less unchanged for so long, creating a real community of flowers and birds, mammals and insects.

53

54

Things to look for in a churchyard

* Birds: foraging among the gravestones for insects; collecting berries from plants such as holly, ivy and yew; or building their nests in tall trees — churchyards are a particular favourite of rooks and jackdaws.

* Mammals: foxes, badgers, squirrels and deer all enjoy the benefits of plenty of food and lack of disturbance.

* Night creatures: owls often favour churchyards, calling from trees or the church tower. Bats, too, are often found here — quite literally nesting in the belfry.

* Wild flowers: many rare wild flowers, now missing from the wider countryside, find sanctuary in churchyards. These include rare orchids and saxifrages. Other commoner wild flowers such as snowdrops and bluebells are also often found there.

* Butterflies: these nectar-rich flowers attract all sorts of butterflies as well as other flying insects.

* Trees and bushes: some of the oldest trees in existence live in our churchyards, with yew trees being particularly ancient.

* Peace and quiet: churchyards are also a wonderful place to sit and appreciate the rich variety of wildlife we share this planet with – go on, try it some time ...

Lichens

Every single churchyard in Britain – whether in the town or country – holds one other ancient secret. For in the midst of death, there is a very special form of life ...

There are things living here that you could quite easily over-look. And yet they're all around us: on the gravestones, on the trees, even on the walls of the church itself. They're not plants, and they're not animals, and they have an amazing lifestyle; and thanks to their great age, an extraordinary story to tell. The name of these organisms? Lichens.

The funny thing about lichens is that although they are every-where, they are so easily overlooked. That's partly because they blend in so well they almost seem to be part of the stone itself.

What exactly are lichens? In your school biology lessons you learn about symbiosis: the working together of two organisms – plants or animals – for mutual benefit. That's exactly what lichens are – a combination of a fungus and an alga. And this partnership certainly does create something truly amazing ...

* Some lichens have been in existence since before the English Civil War, more than three hundred years ago.
* They are among the toughest organisms on the planet, able to cope with extremes of heat and cold that would kill off most other living things.
* They are a really good way of judging air quality – they hate pollution, but thrive in clean air.
* Lichens are used to make all sorts of things, including per-fumes, litmus paper and antibiotic drugs. In the olden days they were often used to dye material in different colours.

A poem about churchyards

The most famous poem written about churchyards – and one of the best-loved poems in the English language – is Thomas Gray's *Elegy Written in a Country Churchyard*, published in 1751. Here are the first few verses:

The Curfew tolls the knell of parting day,
The lowing herd winds slowly o'er the lea,
The ploughman homeward plods his weary way,
And leaves the world to darkness and to me.

Now fades the glimmering landscape on the sight,
And all the air a solemn stillness holds,
Save where the beetle wheels his droning flight,
And drowsy tinklings lull the distant folds.

Save that from yonder ivy-mantled tower,
The moping owl does to the moon complain,
Of such as wand'ring near her secret bower,
Molest her ancient solitary reign …

Three ways to find which direction you are facing without using a compass …

Knowing which direction you are going in isn't just useful – it could save your life, if you are stuck up a mountain in dense fog, for example. So if you're exploring anywhere off the beaten track it's vital to carry a proper compass.

But if you're just off for a walk in the woods, and you get lost, here are three useful ways to find out which direction you're going in without a compass:

1. Use your watch (during the day)

Point the hour hand at the sun. Halfway between the end of the hour hand and twelve o'clock is due south. BUT it is important that you measure the distance going forward in the morning and backwards in the afternoon – so at 8 a.m., the halfway point is 10 a.m.; while at 4 p.m., the halfway point is 2 p.m.

   If it's a cloudy day and you can't see the sun, hold a pen, pencil, or small straight stick, upright on the watch dial. Unless it is really overcast this will cast a faint shadow, so you can work out where the sun is in the sky.

   Of course this method only works with an old-fashioned watch with proper hands – not a digital model!

2. Use the stars (at night)

Find the brightest star in the sky – one that you can see easily. Using a stick, look along its length at the star, as if you're looking down the sight of a gun, and make sure you keep as steady as you can. Wait a minute or two for the star to move.

* If the star has moved left, you are looking north …
* If the star has moved right, you are looking south …
* If the star has moved up, you are looking east …
* If the star has moved down, you are looking west …

3. Use the 'stick-and-shadow' method

(This only works on a sunny day, and does take rather a long time.) Push a straight stick into the ground. Mark the end of the shadow it casts using a small stone or rock, or by scratching a mark in the ground. Keep doing this every hour or so – the place where the shadow is shortest (i.e. closest to the base of the stick) points to the north.

Go out into your garden at night

What could be simpler than to go out into your back garden at night, when it's dark? But you'll be amazed at how different such a familiar place can seem when the sun goes in ...

* Choose a clear night, preferably with a full or nearly full moon.
* Take time getting your eyes used to the darkness, especially if you've just come from a house with all the lights on. One way is to turn out the lights indoors first so you get used to the darker conditions before you go outdoors.
* Don't just look — listen too. While your garden is usually quieter by night than during the day, you may hear nocturnal creatures such as owls hooting; and if you listen carefully enough you may even hear the scratchings of night-time mammals such as voles or hedgehogs.
* Using a pencil torch, lift logs and stones and look under them — there's likely to be all sorts of minibeast activity going on.
* You can take a brighter torch if you want — but remember it might frighten away the creatures you want to see.
* And don't forget to look up at the stars and moon ...

Time thunder and lightning to work out how far away a storm is

Next time there's a thunderstorm, here's a good way to work out how far away the centre of the storm is, and whether or not it's moving towards or away from you.

Using the second hand on your watch (or counting 'one-elephant, two-elephant, three-elephant ...'), work out the time difference between seeing a flash of lightning and hearing the following clap of thunder.

Because light travels almost one million times faster than sound (about 300,000km per second as opposed to about 1,200km per hour), the sound of the thunder takes longer to get to us, even though the lightning and thunder happen at the same time.

The difference between the speed of sound and the speed of light works out at about one kilometre every three seconds (one mile every five seconds) – so if you hear the thunderclap six seconds after seeing the lightning flash, the storm is about two kilometres away …

Count the colours of a rainbow

Do you remember this song? 'Red and yellow and pink and green, orange and purple and blue …'

A lovely lyric, but unfortunately not a very accurate one! The true colours of the rainbow are actually red, orange, yellow, green, blue, indigo and violet … the colours of the visible light spectrum.

Usually the red is on the upper (or outer) part of the rainbow and violet is on the lower (inner) part – but just occasionally a second rainbow is seen outside the first, with the order of the colours reversed.

We see rainbows when the sun is behind us and the rain is in front – the effect is caused by sunlight shining through moisture in the air.

A handy way to remember the order of the colours of the rainbow is: 'Richard Of York Gave Battle In Vain', in which the initial letters of each word represent each of the seven colours.

Skim stones across a lake or pond

One of the most addictive pastimes is to skim a stone across the surface of a river, pond or lake, and see how many times it bounces before losing momentum and sinking into the water. Another name for this game is 'ducks and drakes'. It takes a bit of practice, but here are a few tips on how to play ...

* Find a smooth, flat, oval-shaped stone — it will skim much better than a round or rough one.
* The stone should fit comfortably in the palm of your hand — any bigger and it will be hard to throw properly.
* Throw the stone at an angle of about twenty degrees to the water's surface — that's just a small angle above flat.
* Throw the stone as hard and fast as you can — speed is everything.
* If you can, try to flick your wrist so that the stone is spinning as it leaves your hand — again, this will help maintain its momentum.
* Don't forget to count!

The world record for skimming a stone across the surface of water was set on the Blanco River in Texas in 1992, when Jerdone Coleman-McGhee achieved thirty-eight bounces with a single stone. Then, in July 2007, Russell Byars of Pittsburgh, USA, managed an amazing fifty-one bounces — and he has the video of his feat to prove it!

Play hide-and-seek

You can play hide-and-seek any time and anywhere, so long as there are at least three of you. There are all sorts of varieties, some simple, others complex — but my favourite involves a group of 'hiders' trying to outwit the 'seeker' and get back to base first.

The rules

* Decide the boundaries of the area where you're going to play —
  your garden, your local park, etc.
* Choose something to be your home base: this can be a park
  bench, large tree — anything that's obvious.
* Choose who is going to be the first 'seeker'.
* The seeker closes his or her eyes and counts to ten, twenty or a
  hundred — depending on the age of the children playing the
  game and how far you want them to go.
* The 'hiders' run away and hide.
* The seeker calls out, 'Coming, ready or not!'
* He or she looks out for the hiders as they try to make their way
  back to home base.

* If the seeker sees one of the hiders, he or she should chase and catch them — as soon as they're touched they also become a seeker, trying to find the other hiders.
* Whoever gets to home base first is the winner and will be the seeker in the next game, *unless* nobody gets back to base, in which case the winner is the last person caught. If the seeker doesn't catch any of the hiders, and they *all* get back to home base, he or she is the seeker again.

At the end of the game, there is a tradition that the seeker calls any players who are still hidden using the phrase 'Olly Olly Oxen Free!' The origins of this bizarre custom are lost in the mists of time ...

Visit your local nature reserve

So many people I know would love to visit a nature reserve, but never get around to doing so. Sometimes they just can't be bothered to make the effort, but usually it's because they are simply not sure what to expect.

They worry about things like whether they'll be wearing the right clothes, or carrying the right equipment, or know what to do when they get there. Do they need to bring binoculars or a bird book? Will they be able to get anything to eat and drink? How will they know what to look at?

As a result, they don't go at all, which is a real pity as nature reserves are not difficult places to visit. Here are a few tips:

* Your nearest reserve might be closer than you think: there are thousands of local nature reserves up and down the country, with details available at your local library or on the Internet (just type in 'local nature reserve' and your area into a search engine).

* Organisations such as the RSPB, Wildlife Trusts, Wildfowl and Wetlands Trust and Natural England also run nature reserves and centres all over the country. Again, you can get details of one near you from the organisations themselves or via the Internet.

* Wear something you feel comfortable in – depending on the weather and season, you can wear jeans or shorts, a T-shirt or a fleece, an anorak or a coat, but make sure you have suitable shoes – wear wellingtons or walking boots rather than sandals if it's likely to be wet or muddy.

* If you don't have binoculars borrow a pair from a friend, though many reserves will loan you a pair for a small deposit.

* If you're a real beginner – or even if you're not – sign up for a guided tour. Many larger reserves run regular events led by friendly experts who will be able to point out what's worth looking at and help you identify it.

* Large reserves also have visitor centres where you can buy take-away drinks and snacks or sit down for a light meal, and shops selling everything from books to binoculars – and much more.

Become a conservation volunteer

Once you have become a real wildlife enthusiast – and hopefully you will after reading this book – you may want to give something back to the wild creatures you enjoy watching so much, or to the places you love visiting.

One way to do this is to become a conservation volunteer – doing work at weekends or in your spare time to help conserve or improve wildlife habitats. This is ideal for older teenagers or families.

Volunteering can sound a bit daunting, or perhaps too much like hard work without much reward – but the reality is usually very different. Most people who volunteer find that not only do they give something back to nature, but they also get something out of it themselves.

This can be a practical benefit – many people working full-time in wildlife conservation started off as volunteers – or it may be something less tangible.

Volunteers often talk about an improvement in their quality of life: meeting new friends, getting out in the open air, and feeling fit and healthy are just some of the less obvious benefits. Plus you get to see some great wildlife too!

Ways to volunteer

* Get in touch with one of the big conservation organisations. The RSPB, your local Wildlife Trust and various community projects are always looking for volunteers. You don't need to be an expert: just keen, willing and able to offer a few hours every week or month.
* Check out volunteer organisations such as the British Trust for Conservation Volunteers (BTCV). They have a whole range of opportunities ranging from a day out in your local area, through conservation weekends, to longer holidays – a great way to get involved.
* Ask your friends and their families if they do any volunteering. You may be surprised at how many people already do. First-hand testimony is always the best way to find something that suits you.
* If you don't like the first place you try, don't give up! There are many different projects out there, so you won't necessarily find the perfect fit the first time you try.
* Your school, college or parents' employers may already run a scheme which allows you to do some volunteering. If they don't, maybe you can persuade them to do so.

Use nature to forecast the weather

Red sky at night, shepherd's delight;
Red sky in the morning, shepherd's warning.

This saying isn't just a quaint piece of folklore – it is also surprisingly accurate. That's because when clouds are tinged red by
the setting sun, it means that the air to the west (where most of
our weather comes from) is dry. This generally means the next
day's weather will be fine.

But if the morning sky in the east is red, stormy weather is
usually on the way. This saying is so long-established it can be
found in Shakespeare and the New Testament, and is accurate
roughly seven times out of ten – about the same as a professional
weather forecaster.

This is just one example of our ancestors using natural events
to try to predict the weather – for the next day, month or whole
season. Remember, they didn't have TV or radio weather forecasters, and it was vitally important that they knew what the
weather was likely to do in the coming harvest season or winter
for example.

Some of these techniques are more accurate than others, but
all are worth knowing about, as they can help you understand the
way the natural world is affected by the weather.

So here are a few examples of how you can use your observations of the skies, plants and animals to try to tell what the
weather is going to be like. There are more seasonal examples
later in the book, but here are some more general ones.

* The calls and songs of several birds are supposed to indicate
   rain is on the way. So listen out for the mistle thrush (a loud,
   repetitive song delivered from the top of a tall tree), as this
   means stormy weather is on the way – the bird used to be
   known as the 'stormcock'.
* Another sound that is meant to foretell rain is the laughing
   call of the green woodpecker – known in many parts of Britain
   as the 'rainbird'.

✳ The early arrival of geese in autumn has long been said to foretell a hard winter to come. In fact, birds migrate depending on local weather conditions, and are no better at long-term weather forecasting than we are.

✳ Farmyard animals such as cows and sheep are also sensitive to changes in the weather. Cows are supposed to lie down when rain is on the way, while sheep become friskier or turn their backs to the wind.

✳ Take a close look at the moon — especially a new moon. According to folklore, if the points at each end are turned up, a dry month will follow; if they are turned down, it will be a wet one.

✳ The colour of the moon is also meant to help us tell the weather. A pale moon means rain or snow; a red or orange moon means stormy weather; and a strong, white moon means fine weather, especially in winter — because a strong moon means clear skies, which means fine weather at this time of year.

The direction of the wind is often supposed to indicate the coming weather: broadly wet from the west, warm from the south, cold from the east and dry from the north. But as one rather cynical verse says:

The south wind always brings wet weather.
The north wind wet and cold together;
The west wind always brings us rain,
The east wind blows it back again!

Spring

Nothing is so beautiful as spring —
When weeds, in wheels, shoot long and lovely and lush;
Thrush's eggs look little low heavens, and thrush
Through the echoing timber does so rinse and wring
The ear, it strikes like lightnings to hear him sing.

GERARD MANLEY HOPKINS

We all get excited about the coming of spring, don't we? That's because no other season packs quite so much activity into such a short space of time. Birds are singing, frogs spawning, flowers coming into bloom — and that's just the start. Later on there are baby birds clamouring to be fed, meadows filled with wild flowers, and everywhere you look the sheer exuberance of life — what the poet Dylan Thomas called 'the force that through the green fuse drives the flower'.

Nature's version of spring is a bit more flexible than ours. We usually think of the season starting when the clocks go forward at the end of March — just after the spring equinox — and ending on Midsummer's Day, in the last week of June.

But all this activity couldn't possibly fit into just three months. So the birds in your garden often start singing on fine days in January, while a mild spell in February will bring out the first bumblebees and butterflies. By March some birds have already raised their first brood of young and are starting on another.

At the other end of the scale, the last migrants to return to Britain, the spotted flycatcher and turtle dove, may not arrive here until the middle of May. And birds carry on nesting, flowers keep blooming and insects keep buzzing all the way through the summer, making the end of spring quite hard to pinpoint.

The funny thing about spring is that while it does go on for a long time, certain key activities are tied to particular windows of opportunity — miss them, and you'll have to wait a whole year for another chance.

Look for catkins

My grandmother was born on 11 February 1901; and until she died at the age of ninety, her family would always give her a bunch of pussy-willow catkins on her birthday. Pussy-willow catkins are one of the first signs of life to appear in spring, but it was only years after her death that I discovered why. Because their pollen is carried by the wind, they need to appear before the leaves are on the trees, so that the pollen can travel as far as possible.

Catkins are remarkable things — clusters of tiny flowers, either sticking up like a furry berry (pussy willow) or hanging down like a rather droopy-looking caterpillar (hazel — also known as 'lamb's tails'). They are found on a range of woody plants — including trees such as willow, oak, hazel, birch, poplar, alder and hornbeam.

Catkins are either male or female — though the same tree will often have both. They begin to form in the previous autumn or winter, and then emerge early in the spring — often well before any other signs of life such as buds, leaves or flowers — appear.

hazel

pussy willow

Unlike other flowers, catkins don't have large, brightly coloured petals because they have no need to attract insects to spread their pollen. Instead, they rely on one of the oldest and most reliable forces of nature — the wind.

The best time to find catkins is in January and February. Take a walk through a wood and look for hazel trees, or along a river or stream, where alders or willows grow.

To have a chance of pollinating successfully, catkin-bearing trees produce vast amounts of pollen — a single silver-birch catkin may have as many as five million grains.

Listen for woodpeckers drumming

On a warm, fine day in February or March, listen out for the drumming of woodpeckers. The best places to hear them are woods with plenty of large, old trees.

Just like birdsong, male woodpeckers drum for two reasons: to defend their territory against rival males, and to attract a mate. Of our three species of native woodpecker, by far the most frequent drummer is the great spotted, though green and the rare lesser spotted woodpeckers also drum.

From early spring onwards, the male selects a suitable tree (usually a hollow branch or trunk of a dead or dying one), and then proceeds to drum — producing up to forty blows every second. Just try drumming your fingers at that speed!

You might think that woodpeckers would get a headache from banging their beak against a tree — the equivalent of you or me repeatedly hitting our head against a wall at 26km per hour — but in fact they are superbly adapted to do so.

Woodpeckers have a thick skull, and their brains are very tightly packed inside to reduce the effects of shaking. They also have spongy tissue around their beak which acts like a car's shock absorbers, again minimising the effects of the banging. The eyes are also carefully protected, and are closed just before the beak hits the tree to avoid being damaged by flying bits of bark.

And why don't woodpeckers fall off the tree when they drum? Because they have stiff tail feathers which they wedge against the tree trunk or branch to keep them in place.

Once you've heard the woodpecker drumming, the next step is to try to see it. The earlier in the year you are looking, with fewer leaves on the trees, the better chance you have.

But remember that woodpeckers are shy birds, and that their drumming can carry a long way. So try to approach slowly and quietly, until you're sure you're close to the drumming tree.

Then, taking a stick, beat a rapid rhythm on the tree trunk, trying to reproduce the woodpecker's own sound. With luck the bird will stop drumming and come to investigate what he thinks is a rival male intruding into his territory.

Once you've had a good view, don't confuse the poor chap by beating the stick again, as he needs to get back to drumming to keep hold of his territory.

One British engineer is developing a 'woodpecker hammer' based on the unique way in which a woodpecker drums. The idea is to reproduce the woodpecker's unique method of hammering with very little movement back-and-forth, to create a hammer that can be used in confined spaces.

Find the first spring flowers

What better way to welcome the coming of spring than to take a walk through your local wood and look for the very first wild flowers of the season?

Exactly when you should do this depends on where you are: spring moves up the country gradually from the south and west, so the further north and east you live, the later it will arrive in your neck of the woods. Local climate can make a difference too: plants on high ground come into bloom several weeks later than those in the valleys.

The first flowers usually appear some time in February, though the recent run of very mild winters means that in more sheltered parts of Britain they may be in bloom for the whole of the winter.

The earliest flower – the snowdrop – often appears at the end of January, and has long been associated with the Christian festival of Candlemas, which occurs on 2 February each year.

The link with the Church may have come about because snow-drops often bloom in sheltered churchyards before they appear in the woods.

Another early flower is the crocus – many of these have escaped from gardens, so you shouldn't really think of them as 'wild' flowers. They still gladden the heart on a sunny day in February, though.

Of our truly wild flowers, lesser celandine has always been among the first to appear. The eighteenth-century naturalist Gilbert White gave 21 February as its usual first date, though again this pretty yellow flower may bloom later the further north you live.

Like many woodland flowers, lesser celandines need to bloom early to make the most of the sunshine, as by April or May the tree canopy has closed, and little or no sunlight reaches the forest floor.

During the last week of March, other woodland flowers are also at their best. Carpets of white wood anemones cover the ground – and if you take a closer look at their undersides you can see a lovely pinkish-purple tinge on the petals where they meet the stem. And as spring truly arrives, wild daffodils add a splash of yellow, and the smell of ramsons – wild garlic – hangs in the air.

Although it is sometimes frowned upon, there is no harm in picking a small posy of these early-spring flowers to take home and remind you of your walk in the woods – but never dig up a plant by its roots or pick too many flowers.

In Victorian times, a young lady might send a bunch of snowdrops in an envelope to an overenthusiastic suitor, to remind him of her purity.

The name of one of the earliest spring flowers to appear, primrose, derives from the Latin 'prima rosa' – meaning first rose or first flower.

Flowers which should open on certain saints' days — a list from Richard Inwards' 'Weather Lore' (1893)

2 February: Candlemas	snowdrop
14 February: St Valentine	crocus
25 March: Lady Day	daffodil
23 April: St George	harebell
3 May: Holy Cross	crowfoot
11 June: St Barnabas	ragged robin
24 June: St John the Baptist	scarlet lychnis
15 July: St Swithun	lily
20 July: St Margaret	poppy
22 July: St Mary Magdalene	rose
1 August: Lammas	camomile
15 August: Assumption	virgin's bower
24 August: St Bartholomew	sunflower
14 September: Holyrood	passion flower
29 September: Michaelmas	Michaelmas daisy
25 November: St Catherine	laurel
25 December: Christmas	ivy & holly

Some recipes for spring flowers and plants

When I was a teenager, the naturalist Richard Mabey wrote a book called *Food for Free*, describing all the different ways to get a free meal from the countryside. I can still remember the excitement of realising that all this wonderful food was out there — just waiting to be picked …

How to identify …
wayside and woodland flowers

The phrase 'wayside and woodland' may be an old-fashioned one, but it perfectly describes the kind of flowers we come across on country walks: along the sides of lanes, amongst hedgerows, and in the woods themselves. Many of these are amongst the earliest wild flowers to appear, as they need to bloom before the growth of leaves on the trees makes it too dark for them. So look out for them on country walks anytime from February onwards …

How to identify ...
wayside and
woodland flowers

Lesser Celandine
An early flower, its attractive yellow blooms bring a welcome splash of colour to our woods from February to May. Only opens when the sun shines.

Snowdrop
The first flower to appear, often before the snow has finally melted, this beautiful little plant blooms from January to March, its delicate white flowers drooping from their stems on the woodland floor.

Primrose
The original 'prima rosa', or first flower: the familiar lemon-yellow flowers appear on forest floors and along hedgerows from February to May.

Wild Garlic (Ramsons)
The smell of wild garlic is one of the classic signs of spring in our woodlands. Clusters of spiky white flowers carpet the ground from April to May.

Wood Anemone
Carpets of these little white flowers with their yellow centre cover the forest floor from March to May.

Wild Daffodil
Classic trumpet-shaped, pale yellow flowers with the deeper yellow centre that so inspired the poet Wordsworth. Now only found in scattered sites around the country, as competition from cultivated plants has reduced their range.

Bluebell
Our favourite wild flower, and justly so. The delicate purplish-blue flowers appear from April into June, depending on location, and produce one of our greatest natural spectacles.

Foxglove
One of our best-known and loveliest plants, growing in open woodland and moorland from June to September. Very tall, with a single spike covered with bell-shaped purple or pink flowers.

Violets
A range of closely related wild flowers, appearing from March to May on woodland floors, especially where there is a mixture of dappled sunshine and shade. Range in colour from almost blue to a delicate purple.

Forget-me-nots
Another group of woodland plants, their delicate bluish flowers with yellow centres appearing from spring through to early autumn.

Lily of the Valley
The drooping, bell-shaped, pure white flowers of Lily of the Valley are in bloom from May to June, usually in dry woodland on chalky soils.

Bird's-nest Orchid
This peculiar member of the orchid family obtains all its energy from fungi beneath the soil, and is one of the few plants able to grow in beech woods where sunlight rarely reaches the ground in summer. A single shoot protrudes from the ground, with brownish-yellow flowers.

Unfortunately the idea of collecting, cooking and eating wild plants and other natural things like fungi has pretty much gone out of fashion — buying it from the local supermarket seems so much easier. People are also worried — unduly I think — about the risk of poisoning themselves.

Of course you need to take care and make sure that you know what you're eating. But it's well worth it for the thrill of knowing that you've gone out and foraged for yourself.

Here are a few suggestions for spring food for free:

* Wild garlic: use the flowers or young leaves to add a pungent flavour to salads, or as a garnish on soup. You can even make wild-garlic bread.

❀ Hawthorn: hawthorn leaves can be added to salads or cheese sandwiches, or just munched as you go along on a country walk. The very early bright green buds have a wonderful nutty flavour, and the later darker green leaves taste a bit like parsley.

❀ Stinging nettles: young shoots picked between March and May can be prepared in the same way as spinach or similar greens or made into a tasty and nutritious soup — with lots of iron and as much vitamin C as spinach. But wear gloves to pick them — they sting until they've been cooked.

❀ Wild sorrel: this slightly bitter herb adds a lemony flavour to cooking, and goes well with fish dishes.

The hawthorn was once known as the 'bread-and-cheese tree', because munching on the leaves was supposed to quell hunger pangs as well as a plate of bread and cheese.

Go for a walk in a bluebell wood

A bluebell wood in spring is one of the greatest of our natural spectacles. In fact, about half of all the bluebells in the world occur in Britain, so they are a flower we should be very proud of.

Depending where you live, bluebells usually come into flower some time between late April and mid-May, with the display going on for a few weeks. They need to bloom early, because by mid-May the leafy canopy is beginning to close, blocking out the sunlight which the flowers need to grow.

Most bluebells are found in old woodlands, where the trees are far enough apart to allow the light to reach the forest floor. But you can also see them in other places: along sea cliffs, hedgerows and even roadside verges, especially in the west and north of Britain.

When you visit a bluebell wood, make the most of the experience by first looking at the whole show of flowers. If you half close your eyes, the individual flowers will merge into each other and create a shimmering blue carpet.

Once you've enjoyed the display, take a closer look at the individual flowers themselves. You'll notice they aren't really blue – more a cross between blue and violet, and sometimes almost mauve. They're quite long and narrow, and droop to one side.

If you bend down and get really close you'll notice quite a strong scent. That's to attract the insects which pollinate them – such as bumblebees, which you may be able to spot going from flower to flower on warm, sunny days.

Because people love bluebells so much, they often want them in their gardens, so sometimes dig up wild plants to take home. Rather too many people did this, so that digging them up is now against the law; but if you want to pick a handful of flowers to take home that won't do any harm. Just make sure you don't pull too hard!

You can also wait until the flowers have gone over and collect the dried seeds, then plant them in pots – that way you'll enjoy a home-grown bluebell display the following spring.

Look for squirrel dreys

Wild flowers aren't the only things that are easier to see before the leaves are on the trees. Squirrel dreys – the equivalent of a bird's nest – are also easier to spot at this time of year.

A grey squirrel's drey is an untidy structure, built high up in a tree. It's about the size of a large football, and made of twigs and lined with grass, bark and moss. Unlike birds' nests, the twigs often still have the leaves attached, giving the drey its rather messy appearance. They also have a roof, whereas birds' nests don't.

If you're not sure whether what you've found is a drey or a crow's nest, it's worth waiting a while. On warm, sunny spring days the squirrels will usually be active, and after a while you should see them coming and going to and from the drey.

On warm days you may also see signs of courtship, as one or more males chase the female up and down the trees or along the ground. Once they've mated, the female squirrel carries the babies for about six weeks, giving birth later in the spring. She usually has about three cubs, but can have as many as nine.

Lots of people don't like grey squirrels – and it's certainly true that they don't really belong here, having been introduced from North America by our ancestors in Victorian times. It's also true that they do harm other creatures – notably the native red squirrel.

On the other hand, they are the only furry wild animal that most city kids – and many country ones – will ever see; and watching them as they climb acrobatically around the branches of trees or scamper up a trunk is always good fun.

In parts of Cambridgeshire, Hertfordshire and Bedfordshire, look out for 'black squirrels'. These are not a separate species, but a rare dark form of the grey squirrel, with a sleek black and dark brown fur.

Red squirrels are now quite rare in Britain, as a result of competition from the greys, with their main strongholds being in the pine forests of the Scottish Highlands and the Lake District. However, small populations of this beautiful animal can still be seen on the Isle of Wight, Brownsea Island in Dorset, Formby on the Lancashire coast and in the city parks of Dundee.

Listen to the dawn chorus

It's the best free sound show in the world — yet most people have never even heard it. That's because the dawn chorus starts well before most of us get up — roughly an hour before sunrise. In late spring, the peak time for birdsong, that's about half past three in the morning.

But believe me, if you make the effort to get out of bed, you'll experience something you'll never forget — a whole orchestra of birds, each singing their heart out.

We may think the birds are singing just for us, but the truth is even more interesting. These are all male birds and, for them, singing is a matter of life or death. They're defending their territory against rival males and, at the same time, trying to impress the local females.

So when you hear a robin, blackbird or thrush burst into song, what he's really saying is, 'Oi! This is my space — so get out!' or 'Hello darling ... I'm ready for love — are you?'.

If you want to enjoy the dawn chorus for yourself, here's what you need to know ...

* The peak time for birdsong is late April to mid-May, so that's the best time to be out and about. But birds also sing from mid-February to the end of June, so any time in this period is OK.
* Check sunrise times (using a diary or the Internet).
* If you can, choose a still, clear and fine morning — birdsong carries better when it's not windy. Birds do sing in the rain but you'll get rather wet ...
* Birds sing everywhere — good places to go are your garden, neighbourhood park or local wood.
* Wrap up warm — it can be very cold when you're standing about.
* Take a hot drink and something to eat.
* Keep quiet — otherwise you won't hear what's going on.

* Don't worry about identifying every bird — just relax and enjoy the experience. Later, as the sun comes up, you can try to spot the birds and put a name to each songster.
* If you prefer to go with the experts, the RSPB and local wildlife trusts run regular dawn-chorus walks, usually in the month of May — check out their websites for details.

And if you really can't be bothered to get up so early, just open your window before you go to sleep, add an extra duvet or blanket to keep you warm, and set your alarm for 4 a.m. — then enjoy the dawn-chorus orchestra from the comfort of your bed.

More than two hundred different kinds of bird breed in Britain. The commonest is the wren, with about 10 million pairs.

The earliest bird to sing in the morning is usually the blackbird, closely followed by the robin and song thrush.

Listen for the first cuckoo of spring

Like many people, I heard cuckoos when I was a child, but never saw one. Then, when I was about fifteen, I spent a few days birdwatching at Stodmarsh, near Canterbury in Kent. Cuckoos were everywhere — perched on bushes, uttering their incredible call, and flying through the air like some weird bird of prey. I later discovered that the cuckoo has evolved to look like a falcon or hawk to frighten small birds off their nests, so she can lay her eggs there.

Cuckoos often get a bad press — and with good reason. Unlike any other British bird, they lay their eggs in other birds' nests, letting the foster-parents do all the work. As a result, their youngster gets all the attention it needs, while their foster-parents' eggs and chicks are unceremoniously thrown out of the nest to die.

So why do cuckoos do this? The answer is simple. By taking no part in the raising of their offspring, female cuckoos can lay up to twenty-five eggs – far more than they could ever hope to hatch and raise if they did all the work themselves. As a result, the young cuckoo never meets its real parents, and must fly all the way to Africa on its own – one of the great miracles of nature.

British cuckoos have three main 'host species': reed warbler, meadow pipit and dunnock. Interestingly, a cuckoo will always stick to the same host species to which it was born – so a cuckoo raised by reed warblers will lay its own eggs in reed warblers' nests, and so on.

Such is the mystery and folklore attached to the cuckoo that it has become one of the iconic sounds of spring – a sign that winter is finally over. Considering that cuckoos are quite scarce, it's amazing that it is such a well-known sound – perhaps it's because no other bird sounds quite so much like a human voice.

Letter-writers to *The Times* newspaper used to try to be the first to hear the bird, which led to some famous hoaxes as others tried to fool them. The cuckoo's call is easy to imitate, while the collared dove makes a similar sound (though three notes rather than two), so reports of cuckoos calling before April are usually mistaken.

There is so much cuckoo folklore I could probably write a whole book on it. Here are just a few examples.

* When you hear the first cuckoo of spring, you should run in a circle three times for good luck.
* Alternatively, you must put a stone on your head and run until it falls off. Then come back the next day and there will be money underneath the stone.
* By counting the number of calls, you can work out the number of years before you marry, have a child – or, as some people believe, before you die.

- If you hear a cuckoo after the last day of July (which is very unlikely), this will bring bad luck.
- In Devon, on the River Teign, it is said that the cuckoo calls the salmon upstream.

So to hear a cuckoo ...

- Timing is essential: the main arrival of cuckoos is in the last two weeks of April, and they call most frequently until the middle or end of May.
- Visit the right habitat: extensive wetland reed beds (reed warbler) or windswept moorlands (meadow pipit) are the most likely locations for cuckoos.
- In April you may also see and hear cuckoos as they arrive on south coast headlands such as the Isle of Portland in Dorset, Prawle Point in Devon or Dungeness in Kent.
- Bird reserves such as Minsmere in Suffolk and Stodmarsh in Kent are also cuckoo hotspots, especially in late April and early May.

Don't go listening or looking for cuckoos from June onwards — it's too late! Here's just one version of a well-known rhyme describing the cuckoo's habits:

In April come I will
In May I sing all day
In June I change my tune
In July I prepare to fly
In August away I must.

In some parts of the country, 'cuckoo fairs' are held on a particular date in April or early May to welcome back the cuckoo and the coming of spring. In the village of Downton in Wiltshire, on the first Saturday in May, the Cuckoo Princess is ceremoniously crowned by the Cuckoo King.

The strange white stuff you see on plants in spring, known as 'cuckoo-spit', has nothing to do with the bird. It is produced by the nymph (young) of an insect known as a froghopper – a small green creature that protects itself against the warmth of the sun by surrounding itself in a moist blob of froth. The connection with the cuckoo is simply that the froth tends to appear at about the same time as the bird returns from Africa.

Identify different birdsong

Getting to know songs and calls is a bit like learning a foreign language – apparently impossible at first, daunting, and often confusing. No wonder so many people give up at the first hurdle, or don't even bother to start.

But unless you know at least a few sounds of common birds you will miss out on so much – most experienced birders identify at least half the birds they hear on song or call – especially in spring, when birdsong is at its peak.

So here are a few tips on learning the sounds of our common birds – plus some useful mnemonics or memory aids to help you. Hopefully, you'll find that, just like learning a foreign language, once you have mastered the basics things get a bit easier – and a lot more rewarding.

Tips

* Start in February or March when the resident species are in full song, but before the summer migrants have returned – it's less confusing that way.
* Get outdoors early in the day – birds sing most just before and after sunrise.
* Go to the right place: a local park or woodland will be the most productive, but your garden is also a good place to start as you can practise every day.

* Avoid areas with lots of noise from traffic or people.
* Listen first, and then try to track down the bird that's singing and put a name to it.
* Concentrate on three elements – pitch, rhythm and tone:
  · Pitch: is it high or low?
  · Rhythm: fast or slow? Continuous or broken up into phrases? Repetitive or unpredictable?
  · Tone: is it happy or sad? Harsh or musical?

Some useful memory aids

* Great tit: sings a rhythmic song on two notes – 'tea-cher, tea-cher, tea-cher …'
* Blue tit: a rather unexciting series of high-pitched notes – 'see-see-see-see-see …'
* Robin: sweet, plaintive song delivered in short, apparently random phrases.
* Blackbird: much deeper and fruitier than other birds; also in short, deliberate phrases.
* Song thrush: repeats every phrase several times, using two or three notes at a time – 'Get up, get up, get up; go to bed, go to bed, go to bed …'
* Wren: delivers an astonishingly loud series of phrases with trills and whistles, ending on a flourishing trill.
* Dunnock: a rather odd little song which doesn't seem to have a definite start or end.
* Starling: bizarre series of whistles and metallic tones – more like a machine than a bird; may also mimic anything from car alarms to mobile phone tones.
* House sparrow: an unassuming series of chirps; not really a song as such.
* Pied wagtail: loud, two-note call as it flies off – sounds like 'Chis-ick!'
* Chaffinch: a series of notes descending the scale and speeding up towards the end – has been compared to a cricketer running up to deliver a fast ball.

- Goldfinch: like tinkling bells – very pleasing to the ear.
- Greenfinch: full of harsh, metallic sounds – not very pleasing to the ear.
- Chiffchaff: sings its own name in short phrases – 'chiff-chiff-chaff-chiff-chaff ...'

Go pond-dipping

As kids, on fine days in spring, we would take our nets and jam jars down to the local ford known as the 'watersplash', or the ponds around the local gravel pits, and look for whatever we could find. We weren't fussy – we'd collect everything from tiddlers to water boatmen, from frogspawn to newts, and even the occasional leech. Beneath the surface of even the most ordinary bit of water there is a wondrous variety of hidden life.

Pond-dipping is one of those activities which, although it takes a bit of effort to prepare, is really worth it. Looking a dragonfly nymph straight in the eye, watching a pond skater as it whizzes across the surface, or catching your first stickleback, is a truly wonderful experience.

When to go

Pond life really gets going in spring – though some creatures such as frogs begin their life cycle in January or February by laying their spawn. The best months are from April to June, when most creatures are at their peak of activity, and the layer of algae that covers ponds later in the summer hasn't taken hold yet.

What to take

- A bucket or large plastic container (not glass as it might break) – large empty ice-cream tubs are really good as you can see the creatures more easily against the white background.
- Wellingtons if you don't want to get your feet wet.
- Fishing nets – one each.
- A magnifying glass to take a closer look at whatever you catch.

Tips

- Before you start, take a good look at your pond to see what's there – if you begin dipping too quickly you might frighten everything off.
- Put some clean water from the pond into your container.
- Start by sweeping your net as carefully as you can across the surface of the pond, the rim just beneath the water. This will scoop up any creatures that live on, or just below, the surface.
- Once you've done a couple of sweeps, turn the net inside out over the container. Try not to squash any of the creatures – some are very small and delicate.
- You can also dip your net deeper, to collect things like water snails, tadpoles and perhaps a newt or dragonfly larva.
- Now try to identify what you have caught ...

If you're really keen, lots of wildlife and conservation organisations run pond-dipping events at their nature reserves. (See back of book for details.)

What to look for

- Fish: the commonest are minnows and sticklebacks – under the collective name 'tiddlers'.
- Amphibians: depending on the time of year, you may find frogs or newts at various stages of growth, tadpoles, or even spawn.

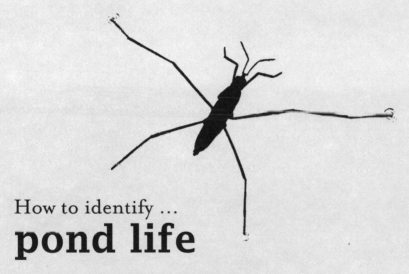

How to identify ...
pond life

Dip beneath the surface of a pond and you'll be amazed at what you find. Insects and their larvae, crustaceans, molluscs and all sorts of other minibeasts can be found here. Identifying them can be a full-time job, and the best way to do so is to use a 'key', which takes you through their features until you eliminate all possible species confusion and arrive at the right answer. But in the meantime, here is a guide to some of the more common freshwater creatures you are likely to find.

How to identify ...
pond life

Pond Skaters

These bizarre little insects are able to use the surface tension of the water to support themselves, enabling them to 'skate' from one place to another. Look for them on the surface of still ponds.

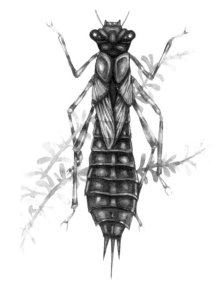

Dragonfly nymphs

These fearsome creatures are the 'big cats' of the pond: ruthless, lethal predators able to seize and eat smaller creatures with ease. May be found either at the bottom of a pond or on plants. In spring, watch as they emerge by climbing up a plant stem, spreading their wings and eventually flying off as an adult dragonfly.

Water Boatmen

These small, dark insects swim around in ponds looking for food, often taken from the bottom. Some species, known as 'backswimmers', move around on their backs, as their name suggests.

Caddis Fly Larvae

There are almost two hundred different kinds of caddis fly in Britain, almost all of which begin life as larvae under the waters of ponds and streams. Look out for this tiny creature hiding beneath a rock, and surrounded by a 'case' of tiny stones and bits of debris, which it uses to protect itself.

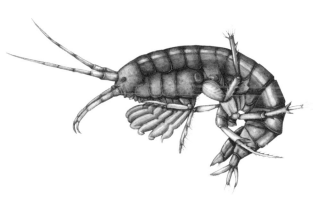

Leeches

If you're pond-dipping this is the creature to avoid! Leeches attach themselves to the skin of fish (and human beings), pierce the flesh and feed on blood. They come in a range of shapes, sizes and colours, but are generally broader at the rear end, tapering to a narrow head and mouth.

Freshwater Shrimps

These tiny crustaceans prefer flowing water such as that found in rivers or streams. They look very like the shrimps we find in rock pools at the sea.

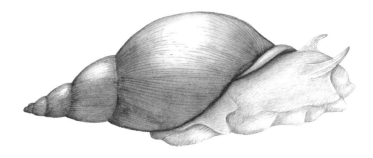

Pond Snails

There are many aquatic varieties of snail living in our ponds, streams and rivers, ranging from tiny species smaller than your fingernail to the giant pond snail, which grows to about the length of your thumb.

- Minibeasts: on or just under the surface, look out for pond skaters (which use the surface tension of the water to support them), water boatmen and various kinds of water beetle.
- Water snails: you should find lots of different kinds, in all sorts of shapes and colours.
- Shrimps: not pink (they only turn that colour when they're cooked) but brown.
- Monsters: dragonfly nymphs are fearsome-looking creatures which will feast on any unfortunate creatures that stray into their territory.
- Nasties: watch out for leeches – the original bloodsuckers …

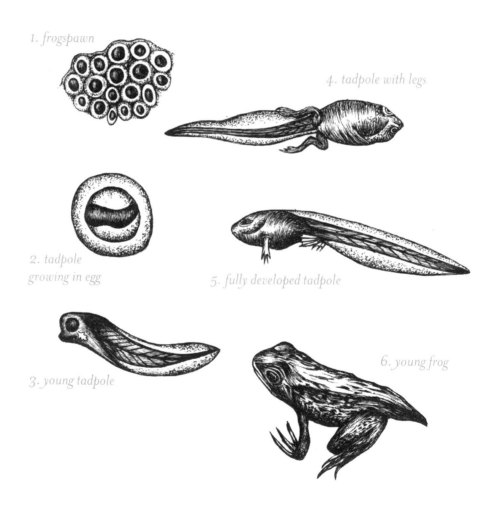

1. frogspawn

4. tadpole with legs

2. tadpole growing in egg

5. fully developed tadpole

3. young tadpole

6. young frog

Collect frogspawn –
and watch them change into frogs

Have you ever wondered how a small ball of jelly with a black dot in the middle turns into a tadpole, then grows legs and arms and becomes a frog?

This truly is one of nature's miracles – and you can watch it happen.

You'll need

* A large glass jar.
* A fishing net (or your bare hands).
* A glass tank (at least 18 by 12 inches).
* A pond or marshy area with some frogspawn in it (depending where you live, frogspawn can be laid any time between January and April).

Tips

* Half fill your jar with water from the pond.
* Scoop up some spawn in your net or hands – making sure you don't squeeze it too hard. Always leave plenty of spawn in the pond to hatch naturally.
* Put it in the jar and take it home.
* Carefully pour the frogspawn into your tank. (Make sure you've cleaned the tank with warm water first.)
* Top up the tank with a bucket of water from the same pond. Don't use tap water as it's full of chemicals which may kill the tadpoles when they hatch.
* Put your tank somewhere cool and safe: such as a garage or shed; or, if you put a cover on it, outdoors.

Frogspawn takes a week or so to hatch into tadpoles. Just like fish, tadpoles breathe through little holes in their sides called gills, and swim as soon as they hatch.

You can feed your tadpoles on water weed, but they also love chopped lettuce. Boil it for a few minutes to make it soft, and chop it up really small. Or you can buy goldfish food from the local pet shop.

Don't feed them too much — and clear away any food they don't eat, otherwise it will go rotten and make the water smell.

Keep looking closely at your tadpoles as they get bigger. After about seven weeks you'll notice tiny bumps on their sides as their back legs start to appear.

A few days later, the same will happen at the front, and soon your tadpoles will have four legs and start to look a bit more like frogs.

At this point, put a rock or two into the tank, so the baby frogs will have something to climb on to as they grow.

Over the next week or so the tail will be reabsorbed into the body, getting smaller and smaller, and finally disappearing altogether. Your tadpoles have turned into froglets. Instead of breathing through gills, they are using their lungs — just like we do.

Now it's time to let them go — ideally in the same pond where you found the frogspawn in the first place.

A typical frog will lay about two thousand eggs every year — of which only a tiny fraction will grow into adult frogs.

It's easy to tell the difference between the spawn of frogs, toads and newts. Frogspawn appears in familiar clumps — looking like the tapioca that used to be served at school dinners. Toads lay their spawn in long 'strings'; while newts just lay single eggs which they hide beneath aquatic vegetation.

How to identify …
frogs, toads and newts

Britain's tally of amphibians is not very impressive: just nine species, three of which were introduced from abroad. Of these, there are four species of frog, two kinds of toad and three types of newt. All breed in water, but spend much of their life cycle on land – characteristic of all the world's 5,700 or so amphibian species.

And just like amphibians everywhere, Britain's frogs, toads and newts are under threat. The main problem is loss of habitat – the number of ponds in Britain has fallen dramatically in the past fifty years or so, as more and more wetlands are drained for farming, or to build homes or roads. Disease is another problem, as is pollution. So if you do come across any amphibians, make sure you don't disturb them – they need all the help they can get.

frogs, toads and newts

Common Frog
The most familiar British amphibian is also one of the most threatened – in fact, it only survives in some areas thanks to garden ponds, which provide a welcome refuge for the frogs to lay their spawn in early spring. Can vary in colour: but usually a combination of green, brown or yellow marked with dark blotches, including a distinctive mask across the eyes. Moves by hopping, using its powerful hind legs.

Edible Frog, Pool Frog and Marsh Frog
These species were all introduced from Continental Europe during the twentieth century, and are now thriving in many parts of south-east England – perhaps as a result of climate change. They are very similar-looking bright green frogs, generally detected by their incredibly loud and far-carrying calls, especially in the breeding season.

Common Toad
Although superficially similar in size and shape, toads can easily be told apart from frogs by their warty skin, darker colour and habit of walking instead of hopping. Will make long journeys to get to their breeding grounds, often crossing roads or paths, where they can easily fall victim to passing traffic.

Natterjack Toad

This rare relative of the Common Toad is confined to a few sandy heaths in southern England and parts of the north-west. Best told apart from its commoner relative by the distinctive yellow stripe down the centre of its back. Can often be heard calling at night.

Great Crested Newt

The largest and scarcest British newt, the male is a magnificent creature, with a jagged crest along the length of his back and a bright orange belly. Females are less obvious, but still brightly coloured.

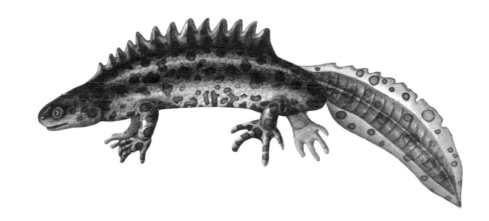

Smooth and Palmate Newts

These two newts are not easy to tell apart, especially outside the breeding season. Both are smaller and less well marked than the great crested, though breeding males can show an orange belly and appear quite brightly coloured.

Go on an Easter-egg hunt

Easter is one of the best times of year for getting out and about in your garden or local park, or taking a walk through the woods. One way to make it a bit more fun is to organise an Easter-egg hunt.

    The rules are very simple. One person hides the eggs and works out clues to help the others (any number from two to twenty) to find them.

These clues can be in the form of a rhyme, for example:

An egg's an object without an edge,
So look for it in the garden hedge …

Or a puzzle:

Clue: The next egg is hidden in a place that rhymes with marrow.
Answer: Wheelbarrow!

If you can't find an egg after a few minutes, ask for more clues. If you're really struggling, get them to say 'Warm, warmer ...' if you're getting close, or 'Cold, colder ...' if you're looking in the wrong place.

If there are younger children with you, make sure you let them find some of the eggs themselves, by giving them easier clues.

Like many Christian customs, giving eggs at Easter time goes back beyond the birth of Christ to pagan times. Eggs are thought to symbolise the new life brought by spring.

Dye your Easter eggs yellow using gorse flowers

A friend of mine tells me that when she was growing up she and her friends would collect saucepans full of gorse flowers and boil them up with hen's eggs (*not* chocolate ones!) to make them turn a cheerful yellow.

This is her recipe

* Take a bucket or a large saucepan and fill it full of gorse flowers — being careful not to graze yourself on the prickles of the bush (you may want to wear gardening gloves).
* When you get home, cover the blossoms with water, bring to the boil and gently simmer for about ten minutes until the water turns yellow.

- Then add the eggs (if you can get hold of some, white ones are best as they colour better than brown), and boil for another ten minutes or so.
- Carefully remove the eggs from the saucepan, dry them off with a piece of kitchen towel, and put them in an egg carton to cool.
- Once they are cool, use poster paints to decorate them.

And try these alternatives to gorse flowers for different colours

- Ripe blackberries (purple).
- Nettles (green).
- Beetroot (reddish purple).

An old country proverb says that 'when gorse is in flower, kissing is in season'. And because gorse is almost always in flower, you can kiss at any time of year …

Have a snail race

My mother was never a big fan of snails – in fact, she fought a running battle with them as they chomped and munched their way through her prized plants. But as I used to point out to her, snails do have their uses – if only as food to attract song thrushes and hedgehogs to the garden. So if you take a more tolerant attitude, and don't mind a few leaves with holes in them, then snails are one of the most fascinating garden creatures …

Snail racing is something you can do in your garden any time from May until September, when there are plenty of snails. It's a great thing to do with two or three friends.

First, collect your snails – choose the largest ones you can find – and pop them in a bucket with a few lettuce or cabbage leaves to keep them going.

Then you need to make a racetrack. Because snails can't be easily persuaded to go in one direction, the best way to do this is to get a large piece of wood, at least four feet across, with a smooth surface. Using a marker pen, draw a small circle in the centre; and another, much larger circle on the outer edges.

When you are ready, put your snails in the centre circle. Then just watch them go! Make sure you know which snail belongs to which person, so you can cheer your own one on.

You can either have a time limit (say twenty or thirty minutes), after which the winning snail is the one furthest from the centre circle, or just let the race go on until the winning snail has crossed the outer circle line.

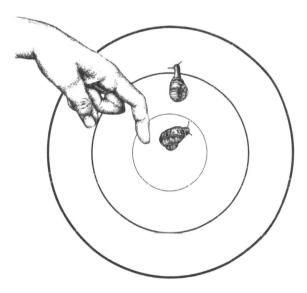

Another way to see how fast snails travel is to mark the shells of those in your garden using Tipp-Ex (the stuff we used to use to correct typing errors in the days before computers). By marking individual snails with different patterns you'll be able to identify which one has moved furthest in a single day or night.

Snails are not known for their speed, but the speckled garden snail can move as much as fifty metres per hour. This is about 6,500 times slower than a Formula One racing car, and about 150 times slower than human walking pace.

Identify trees by their leaves

Spring is a wonderful time to get to know trees. As they come into leaf they adopt their familiar appearance and are generally easier to identify than at other times of the year.

The key place to start is by deciding what kind of leaf you're looking at. First try to work out if it comes from a broad-leaved tree such as oak, ash or horse chestnut, or a coniferous tree such as pine or larch. Then sort different leaves into shapes.

* Jagged: e.g. sycamore, London plane.
* Heart-shaped: e.g. lime, black poplar, birch.
* Lobed: e.g. oak, hawthorn.
* Oval-shaped: e.g. sweet chestnut.

Finally, try to match up individual leaves with the guide – you can also use other clues such as the bark, flowers, etc.

Why trees (and other plants) have leaves ...

* Trees need leaves to get their energy – by a process known as photosynthesis.
* It works like this: plants capture the energy from the sun using a substance in their leaves called chlorophyll (which also makes leaves green).

How to identify ...
trees

Our grandparents' and great-grandparents' generation could put a name to most of the trees they would see in the country-side; but in the past few decades we seem to have lost this rich store of knowledge. Many people today walk through a wood unable to tell which trees they're passing; which is a pity, because once you can put a name to a tree you can also learn a lot more about it and the wild creatures that depend on it.

To identify which tree you're looking at, it's best to use a range of different features. For some, like the oak and horse chestnut, the leaves are really distinctive; while for others, like the beech, the overall shape of the tree also helps you. Buds, seeds and fruits, and the bark are also good ways of telling one tree from another.

How to identify ...
trees

Oak

One of the best known of our native trees: large and long-lived, with a characteristic 'bushy' shape due to twisted branches. Leaves are quite long with irregular edges known as 'lobes'. In autumn, look out for acorns.

Beech

Another much-loved native tree: often very tall, with a smooth, grey trunk. Branches start quite high up, and leaves are so dense the forest floor is often clear because very little can grow beneath the canopy. In autumn, look for the tree's nuts, known as 'beechmast', which come in spiny cases.

Ash

A tall, grey tree with slender branches giving an 'open' appearance. Look out for leaves appearing in pairs along a stem, sticky black buds in spring and bunches of 'keys' (the wind-blown seeds) which appear in autumn.

Horse Chestnut

The tree we all know and love for the fruit it provides every autumn: conkers. Leaves are very distinctive, divided into six or seven separate parts. In spring, the flowers appear in showy whitish-pink bunches; then, in early autumn, come the conkers in their green prickly cases.

Sweet Chestnut

Famous for its edible and very tasty fruit – the nuts that appear every autumn. The tree itself is quite tall and slim, with dark brown bark. The long leaves have jagged edges. Nuts come in a case with small, dense spines.

Elm

Much rarer now because of Dutch elm disease, which killed off virtually all mature trees. May still be seen as young trees in hedgerows: look for oval leaves with jagged edges.

Sycamore

A common and widespread tree, introduced here many centuries ago from southern Europe. Has large, distinctive leaves, which are divided into five parts, and very dense foliage. Tall, with a rounded outline. In autumn, look out for the 'winged' fruits which are spread by the wind.

Lime

One of our tallest and most impressive trees, with distinctive heart-shaped leaves and fat, juicy buds. Often planted in city streets and parks, as it is tough and long-lived.

Willow

The 'weeping willow' is one of our most familiar trees, with slender, golden-yellow twigs and pale green leaves hanging down in bunches, almost reaching the ground. Yellow, drooping catkins appear in spring. Usually found near water.

Silver Birch

Best identified by the pale, silvery-white bark that gives the tree its name, and peels away easily to reveal the dark wood beneath. Tall and slender, with drooping branches and leaves, and catkins in winter and early spring. Often found near water.

Norway Spruce

The classic 'Christmas tree', though if left can grow much larger than the one in your front room! Tall, slender and often triangular in shape, with long shoots covered with the short, slender needles.

Scots Pine

Our largest native conifer, widespread in Scotland but has also been planted in many other locations. Very tall and majestic, with reddish-brown bark and distinctive 'needles' (in fact, these are leaves which have adapted to retain water all year round). Produces pine cones — each segment protecting a tiny, wafer-thin seed.

Alder

Almost always found by water, this medium-sized tree has rather irregular oval-shaped leaves, and produces long, drooping catkins in early spring, as well as small, black cones.

- They then combine it with carbon dioxide (from the air) and water (from the soil via the roots) to make glucose and oxygen.
- The plant can then convert the glucose into sucrose, and send it to the stem, leaves, etc.; or into starch, to be stored for future use.
- The oxygen (a waste product from the plant's point of view) is excreted for us to breathe. Without this waste oxygen, animal life on the planet – including us – could not survive.

Dig for earthworms

The humble earthworm must surely be the most underrated creature on the planet. Charles Darwin certainly thought so. He called them 'nature's plough', and pointed out that without worms' ability to process decaying vegetation and get air into the soil, the world as we know it would not exist: 'All the fertile areas of this planet have at least once passed through the bodies of earthworms.'

Worms are vital to the health of soil in your garden, and also provide food for everything from robins to hedgehogs, including moles, beetles and even snails.

To dig them up, you'll need

- A small gardener's fork or trowel.
- A plastic tray or box where you can put the worms.
- A magnifying glass.

The best time to look for earthworms is after a shower or longer spell of rain, when they'll come to the surface of the soil, making them easier to find. But they won't stay above ground for long, as they are easy prey for birds such as blackbirds and song thrushes, so you may need to dig in the soil to find them.

Use a small gardener's fork, which allows you to turn over the soil gradually and find worms as you go, so you're less likely to damage them. If you do cut a worm in two it can regenerate itself, but you should still avoid harming them if you can.

Once you've collected a few worms in a plastic tray or box, take a close look, using a magnifying glass. You'll notice that their body is made up of tiny rounded segments, joined together to allow the worm to move around by expanding and contracting its body. The front end is the one with the bigger segments making a bulge.

The earthworm's mouth is more or less invisible — but it does exist. As they eat, the food passes straight into their digestive system, where it decomposes and is passed out the other end.

Look for mad March hares

The March hare … as this is May, it won't be raving mad — at least not so mad as it was in March.

ALICE'S ADVENTURES IN WONDERLAND, LEWIS CARROLL

We often hear someone described as 'mad as a March hare', or 'hare-brained' — but where did these strange phrases come from?

As with so many things in nature, it all comes down to love. In early spring, male hares (known as 'jacks') start to get a bit frisky, and chase the females ('jills') around the fields, hoping to mate with them.

But the females don't give in that easily. They will often face up to their pursuer, and try to fend him off. Sometimes the male and female will stand up on their hind legs and 'box' each other with their front paws.

Our ancestors were so baffled by this extraordinary behaviour they assumed that hares go mad at this time of year — hence the phrase 'mad March hare'.

Female hares can have up to three litters of young a year, giving birth to four young, called 'leverets', at a time.

The brown hare (to give it its full name) is nothing like as common or widespread as the rabbit, and in the past few years has declined more rapidly than any other British mammal, apart from the water vole.

But hares can still be found where traditional farming methods are practised, especially in the east of England and Scotland. Wiltshire, Hampshire, Hertfordshire, Norfolk and Lincolnshire are all good counties for hares.

Tips

- Early spring (February to April) is the best time to search for hares, as the grass is shorter so they're easier to see; they are also a lot more active at this time of year.
- Like many mammals, hares are easiest to see at dawn and dusk.
- Seek out traditionally farmed fields with short cropped grass, crops or ploughed earth, where the hares can run around; and which are surrounded by hedgerows.
- Scan the fields using binoculars – for such a large creature, hares can be surprisingly hard to see – and look for the black tips of their ears.
- Don't get too close or make any sudden movements as this will frighten the hares: either crouch down behind a hedge, or stay in the car – which makes an excellent hide!

How to tell a hare from a rabbit ...

- Hares are much larger, with longer ears which have black tips.
- When hares run, their longer legs are really obvious.
- Hares are paler and more yellowish in colour than rabbits, which are usually darker brown.
- Rabbits live in burrows; hares don't.
- If they're boxing, they're hares!

Watch spring lambs

Spring is lambing time in many parts of Britain – especially the hillier north and west. And nothing signals the coming of the new season like seeing newborn lambs gambolling in the fields.

Look out for spring lambs any time from January to June, depending on where you live. They usually appear much earlier in the milder south-west, and latest of all in the hillier parts of the Lake District and Scotland. There it can still snow as late as May – known locally as the 'lambing snows', as this can be a treacherous time for the young animals.

To see lambs at really close quarters, visit one of the many farms across Britain which open up to the public and let you come in and watch the animals.

Find a bird's nest

Egg-collecting is now against the law, and for very good reason. Birds have enough problems to deal with in the breeding season without having to lay their clutch of eggs again because someone has raided their nest.

But the one good thing to be said about 'birds-nesting', as it used to be called, was that it gave you a really good understanding of what birds actually do in their day-to-day lives.

Finding birds' nests is not as easy as it sounds – most are hidden away in dense vegetation, to stop predators finding the precious eggs or chicks – and learning how to spot them gave many older birdwatchers a really good apprenticeship in getting to know various different species.

There is nothing wrong with looking for nests, just don't disturb the occupants. Here are some tips on what to look for, when and how.

Timing

* Most birds breed in spring – though in the bird world that can start as early as January (and possibly before Christmas during mild winters) and go on into late summer or even autumn.
* So the best time to look for nests is March or April – before the leaves on trees and bushes have had time to grow and hide them from view.
* Remember that some birds don't come back from Africa until April or May – so don't look for swallow or house martin nests too early.

Where to look

* Start by keeping your eyes open when you're on a walk or bike ride. Look at different levels – some birds like robins and wrens nest very low down in vegetation like brambles; others, like crows and magpies, nest high in the top of a tree.
* Some nests are really obvious, such as those built by rooks – in a colony high in tall trees known as a 'rookery'. Rooks start nesting in February, and until the trees come into leaf you can easily find and watch them. The only downside is that you can't actually see inside the nests as the nests are usually far too high.
* Other really obvious nests are those made by house martins – which as their name suggests are built on the side of a house, just beneath the eaves. In May you can watch house martins build (or rebuild) their nests using tiny balls of mud.

What to look for

✤ Not all nests are the same size and shape. Some, like those made by small birds such as thrushes and robins, are neat, cup-shaped structures lined with grass or mud. Others, like that of the magpie, are a rough assembly of sticks in the branches or twigs of a tree.

✤ Many birds, including tits and woodpeckers, nest out of sight in holes in trees — where they and their eggs and chicks can be safe from predators. Although you can't see the nest itself, you can sit and watch the birds flying in and out — especially once the chicks have hatched and the parents need to bring thousands of caterpillars to feed them.

✤ Some birds — especially robins, pied wagtails and blackbirds — often make their nests in really unusual places. Odd nest sites have included a teapot, under the bonnet of a working Land Rover, the coat pocket of a gardener (while he had hung it up in his tool shed between breakfast and lunch) and even (a long time ago) in the skull of a hanged man.

How to find a nest

✤ By far the best way to find a nest — and to learn more about the bird and its habits — is to sit quietly in a suitable spot and watch the behaviour of the birds you see.

- Look out for birds carrying nesting material such as grass, leaves or twigs (early in the season) or food for chicks (later on).
- Parent birds will also remove the chicks' droppings in a 'faecal sac' — memorably described by Bill Oddie as 'shrink-wrapped poo'.

Looking for nests on water

- Waterbirds such as ducks, swans, grebes, coots and moorhens often build their nest in full view, a few feet out into the water. To stop it floating away they attach it to an underwater plant.
- If the nest is close enough to the bank you should be able to see the eggs, and when the chicks hatch you can watch them being fed by their parents.
- The chicks of most waterbirds are 'precocial', which means they are able to swim — and to some extent fend for themselves — almost as soon as they hatch. But you can usually track them down by listening for the sound of tweeting as they anxiously call to remind their mum and dad that they're still here …

How you can help

- If you do find a bird's nest, be careful not to disturb it. Put any foliage you've moved back into position, and move away as quickly as possible so as not to attract the attention of predators or upset the parent birds.
- In spring, put out hair (of pets, horses or humans) or bits of wool, straw and grasses for the birds to use to line their nest.
- Make a nest box. (See Autumn.)
- Put out live food such as mealworms to help parent birds feed their hungry young — especially in wet weather when they need all the help they can get.

Many birds could not thrive in spring without the help of spiders. Not only do the spiders provide nutritious food for the adults and their chicks, but spiderwebs are used in the construction of many species' nests.

Long-tailed tits make spectacularly intricate nests in which spiderwebs play a central role. They spend three weeks creating their nest out of moss, held together by sticky cobwebs, and then cover the outside of their new abode with lichen as camouflage. As a finishing touch to make it extra comfy, they then fill the nest with up to 2,000 downy feathers — just like snuggling into a luxury duvet!

Visit a rare bird watchpoint

Not all that long ago, the whereabouts of rare breeding birds used to be a closely guarded secret, known only to a tiny handful of people. This was to guard against a small but determined band of egg-collectors, who would raid nests and steal the eggs.

But in the past few years conservationists have taken a different view. Nowadays the RSPB believes that if you make the nesting site of a rare bird public, and encourage people to come to see it, it makes it safe — after all, who would be stupid enough to raid a nest which is constantly being watched?

This is great news if you're keen to see some of our most spectacular birds — especially birds of prey like ospreys, peregrines, red kites, and two of our largest and most impressive birds, golden and sea eagles.

During the breeding season — roughly April to August depending on the species — the RSPB organises watchpoints up and down the country, as part of its 'Aren't Birds Brilliant!' scheme.

Birds of prey often nest in the same place year after year, so some of the watchpoints, such as the famous osprey hide at Loch Garten in Scotland's Speyside, are permanently open to the public in spring and summer. Others — including the sea eagles on the Isle of Mull and red kites in Gateshead — are more mobile, so the exact location may vary from season to season.

And these aren't just in remote, wild places: in the past twenty years or so the fastest living creature on Earth, the peregrine, has moved into many of our busiest cities, and can be seen in urban areas throughout Britain.

A hunting peregrine can 'stoop' (dive down towards its prey) at more than 180kph — and possibly as fast as 300kph — roughly the same top speed as a Formula One racing car.

Check out the RSPB's website for details of the best dates and times to visit — and don't worry if you don't have any binoculars, as volunteers are always on hand to help you spot the bird and get good views through powerful telescopes.

Spring weather lore

'March winds and April showers' pretty much sums up the British spring, but our ancestors found plenty to disagree about when it came to using nature to forecast this season's weather.

Starting with the period of fasting known as Lent, which runs for forty days from Ash Wednesday to Good Friday, it was said that:

'Wherever the wind lies on Ash Wednesday, it continues during all Lent.'

At the end of the Lent period, a similar forecast was made:

'Rain on Good Friday foreshadows a fruitful year.'

But another proverb is more ambiguous:

'A good deal of rain upon Easter Day, gives a good crop of grass, but little good hay.'

It's hardly surprising that May Day — the main celebration of the coming of spring — gave rise to all sorts of sayings which try to forecast the weather for the season ahead. Several proverbs suggest that cold weather on May Day will bring a good harvest; while the late flowering of the blackthorn (indicating a cold spring) is supposed to be good news for farmers as well. This may well be true: after all, cold winters help to kill off moulds, pests and diseases — increasing the chances of a bumper crop.

Later in the month, fine weather is hoped for — as shown by another ancient proverb:

'A swarm of bees in May is worth a load of hay.'

But perhaps the best-known spring-weather saying is meant to help us forecast the weather for the summer to come:

'Oak before ash, we're in for a splash; Ash before oak, we're in for a soak.'

This ancient rhyme suggests that if the oak tree comes into leaf before the ash, the summer will be dry; whereas if the ash is the first, a wet summer will follow.

The accuracy of this is open to debate — but what we do know is that the oak, which has generally come into leaf a few days before the ash, is now doing so much earlier than it used to, apparently as a result of climate change.

So if global warming continues to raise spring temperatures, it is increasingly unlikely that we shall ever see the ash coming into leaf before the oak again — which, according to the proverb, means summers will get hotter and drier.

Summer

Sumer is icumen in,
Lhude sing cuccu!
Groweth sed, and bloweth med,
And spring the wude nu ...
ANON

'Summer is coming …' is the oldest known poem written in more or less modern English, and shows our thirteenth-century ancestors' excitement at the arrival of the warmest, sunniest season of all.

Nowadays, summer is the ideal time to get out and about in the countryside, and enjoy the benefits of warm, sunny days and long, light evenings. But as the school summer holidays draw to a close, and autumn begins, how many of us look back and realise we've missed the chance to enjoy all those classic summer pastimes for another year?

Here are dozens of things you can do during the summer months: from watching dragonflies to collecting caterpillars; city safaris to nights in the garden; and a whole host of activities for a summer holiday by the seaside.

So pack the suncream and the sunglasses, butterfly net and binoculars, and get out there and enjoy!

Collect caterpillars and watch them change into butterflies

This is the best way for anyone to learn about the miracle of metamorphosis — one of the most complex and extraordinary processes in nature. And with a little effort you can see it happen before your very eyes …

What you need

- Something to collect the caterpillars in: traditionally a large jam jar with a lid, but plastic food containers such as Tupperware boxes may be more practical. Remember to make small holes in the lid so the caterpillars can breathe.
- Rubber gloves or gardening gloves to pick up the caterpillars. Some caterpillars — especially the big hairy ones — have poisonous hairs (to make them unpleasant for birds to eat) which can irritate your skin.

Collecting your caterpillars

- Look for caterpillars any time between May and August, with the most variety available in June and July.
- Once you find them, gather up a maximum of five and put them into your plastic container, ideally with a stem or two of the plant they are feeding on at the time.
- When you collect the caterpillars, also bring home extra stems of the plant you find them on and keep them fresh in a jug of water. This is known as their 'food plant', and many kinds of butterfly or moth only feed on a single type.
- Never pick up a caterpillar you find on the ground — it is searching for its food plant or wandering off to pupate, and needs to be left alone.

Food plants of some British butterflies

CATERPILLAR'S FOOD PLANT	BUTTERFLY
cabbages, kale and nasturtiums	large white and small white (both also known as 'cabbage white')
stinging nettles	peacock, red admiral, small tortoiseshell, comma
buckthorn & alder buckthorn	brimstone
garlic mustard	orange tip
holly & ivy	holly blue
milk parsley	swallowtail

Looking after them

- ☼ Keep your caterpillars in a tank — you can buy this at any pet shop. Put the stems of their food plant into a small jar of water inside the tank, and bring fresh plant material in every couple of days.
- ☼ Cover the tank with a lid to stop them escaping, but make sure there are enough air holes to keep them alive.
- ☼ It's best to keep your tank in a cool place, otherwise the butterflies will emerge too early — a garage or garden shed is ideal.
- ☼ Make sure you provide a good supply of the food plant as the caterpillars grow — they are voracious eaters. And the bigger they get, the more they eat — some will need new supplies every day.
- ☼ From time to time your caterpillars will shed their skin and emerge looking fresh and new. You may notice bits of shed skin in the tank. When caterpillars change their skin they usually stay still — make sure you don't pick them up at this time.

Tip

Some caterpillars can become cannibals if kept in close proximity with others – especially the caterpillars of the orange tip butterfly, which you might find on garlic mustard in late spring and early summer.

Pupation

Eventually, your caterpillars will have grown to their full size, and at this time they are ready to enter the next stage of their metamorphosis – pupation.

In this incredible process, the caterpillar effectively goes into a state of suspended animation (quite literally, as the pupa or chrysalis hangs from a twig or leaf), while its body is broken down into a kind of mush. It then reconstitutes itself into the next stage, the adult butterfly or moth.

Some caterpillars bury their pupae in damp earth, while others affix themselves to bark – so make sure your tank contains both earth and some old bits of bark, twigs and branches to give them both options.

Pupae that form during the spring and summer generally hatch into butterflies or moths after a month or so; those that form in autumn usually remain in this state throughout the coming winter, and emerge the following spring.

Emergence

When you think the adults are about to emerge it's a good idea to place some more twigs and stems in the tank so they can stretch their wings to dry them after they've come out. Don't be tempted to touch their wings at this stage as you might damage them – just leave the insects alone and they'll sort themselves out.

Once they have emerged and the wings are fully dried and stretched, release the adults into the same area where you found the caterpillars. Watch out for birds, which can make an easy meal of a new butterfly – if possible, hide the insect beneath some foliage so it can't be easily spotted.

Catch butterflies with a net

In Victorian times, thousands of enthusiastic young men and women roamed the countryside armed with a butterfly net, a jar of chloroform, and a box containing corks and pins. They were chasing butterflies, and having caught them they would kill, mount and preserve the fragile creatures in cabinets, so they could show them off to their friends.

For many years now, collecting and killing butterflies has, quite rightly, been discouraged. But there's nothing to stop you using a butterfly net to catch them, so you can take a closer look before releasing them unharmed.

It's best to use a proper butterfly net, which can be bought from specialist dealers for about £20. These have fine mesh and are large enough for you to catch your quarry. You'll also need clear plastic boxes to hold the butterflies in – again, these can be bought from dealers, some with a built-in magnifying lens so you can get really close-up views.

Catching your butterflies

☺ Look for butterflies on a warm, sunny day, from about mid-morning until late afternoon, when they are most active. But be aware that during the middle of the day some butterflies may be a bit too active for you to catch them!

- If there are plenty of nectar-rich flowers, your garden is a good place to start. If not, visit a local park or wood, or a traditional meadow full of wild flowers.
- Check out areas where the sun and shade meet — butterflies often feed along garden borders, footpaths and woodland rides, where there are plenty of flowers.
- Take time to get to know the habits of the butterfly you're chasing — some fly almost constantly, rarely settling; others will stay put for minutes on end, basking in the sunshine.
- Stalk your quarry. Butterflies are very sensitive to movement, so creep up on them slowly and carefully.
- Once you're within range (less than a metre away), bring the net down rapidly on top of the butterfly, being careful not to bash it with the frame.
- You must get the butterfly in the tip of the net, and then fold the net over so it can't escape.

Once you've caught them

- Usually the caught butterfly will flutter its wings for a few seconds, and then stay still. Carefully insert your collecting box under the rim of the net, and persuade the butterfly to enter. Be very careful not to damage its wings. Once the butterfly is safely in the box, slide the lid across to make it secure.
- Then take a few minutes to have a really close look. You'll see how the colour on the wings changes depending on the angle at which you're looking.
- With the help of a butterfly guide you should be able to identify it — there are only about sixty different kinds of butterfly in Britain, of which about a third are really common (see How to identify ... butterflies page 126–7).
- After you've had a good look, release the butterfly in the same place you caught it.

How to identify ...
butterflies

Butterflies are some of our most beautiful and fascinating insects. Their life cycle, in which an egg hatches into a caterpillar,
then turns itself into a chrysalis and finally emerges as a winged
adult, is little short of a miracle.

They are also common (though sadly not as common as they
used to be) and easy to spot — though on fine summer's days they
do fly a bit too fast to get a really close look.

There are around sixty different kinds of butterfly in Britain,
of which about two-thirds are either very scarce or found only in
specialised habitats such as ancient woodlands, chalk grasslands
and mountainsides. But about twenty butterflies are common
and widespread, and likely to be seen either in your garden, or
on a walk alongside a hedgerow or at the edge of a wood. Here's a
guide to telling them apart.

Different butterflies come out at different times of the year —
so if you're not sure what you're looking at, check when it's most
likely to be found.

How to identify ...
butterflies

Small Tortoiseshell
March to October,
almost anywhere
One of our commonest
and most widespread
butterflies, and can be seen
in almost every month as it
hibernates here. Medium-
sized, with classic 'tortoiseshell' pattern of orange
and black, and blue spots
on the edges of the wings.

Comma
February/March to early
autumn, England and Wales
Distinctive orange-and-
black butterfly with crinkly
edges to its wings and a tiny
white mark below that gives
the comma its name. Loves
buddleias.

Peacock
March/April to September, almost anywhere apart from northern Scotland
Stunning creature, with huge 'eyes' on the tips of the
wings which are meant to fool predators and allow the
butterfly to escape from attack. Deep orange, with blue,
yellow and black 'eyes'.

Red Admiral
April/May to September/
October, almost anywhere
One of our largest and
most handsome butter-
flies: basically black and
orange-red with white
markings near the wing
tips. Loves feeding on
fallen fruit. Comes here
each spring from Conti-
nental Europe, migrating
back in autumn.

Painted Lady
May/June to August/September,
mainly in the south
Like a washed-out version
of the red admiral, this
is another migrant, some
flying here all the way from
North Africa. Common in
some summers; very scarce
in others. Look out for a
black and-orange butterfly
with white on the wing tips,
and long wings.

Marbled White
Late June to August,
mainly in the south and west
Not a 'white' at all, but
a 'brown' with white
mottling on its dark wings.
A grassland species some-
times found in gardens.

'Cabbage' White
April/May to August/September, almost anywhere
This is in fact three separate but very similar species: large, small and green-veined
whites. All are white above, with black spots and black edges to their wings; and yellowish
below. Look out for the green-veined white's distinctive underwing pattern of black
streaks on a yellow background.

Clouded Yellow
May to September, mainly in the south
Another migrant, seen in huge numbers in some summers, and other years virtually absent. Resembles the brimstone, but much deeper, richer yellow and with black wing tips.

Brimstone
February/March to late autumn, mainly in England
One of the first butterflies to emerge, sometimes seen on sunny days in late winter, this is the original 'butter-coloured fly'. Male is pale lemon yellow; the female is much paler, and can be confused with one of the 'whites', but has no black on her wings.

Gatekeeper
July to August, grassy areas in the south
Appears later than the meadow brown, and is smaller, brighter and smarter than that species. The orange patches above are more obvious than on the meadow brown, and the underwings are also brighter. 'Eyes' above and below.

Meadow Brown
May to August/September, almost anywhere
Our commonest and most widespread butterfly, but often overlooked because of its rather drab appearance. Males are basically dark brown, with small brown 'eyes' above and below, and orange on the underwings. Females have orange on the upperwings too. Larger than the similar gatekeeper. Prefers long grass.

Orange Tip
April to June, almost anywhere
The male is really easy to spot, thanks to the bright orange patches on his white wings, which also have black tips. The female looks very like the cabbage whites, but her underwings are mottled with green.

Small Copper
May to October, England and Wales
This little gem of a butterfly makes up in beauty what it lacks in size. Dark brownish-grey hindwings with an orange border, and bright orange forewings spotted with brownish grey.

Speckled Wood
April/May to August/September, mainly in the south
A mainly dark brown butterfly with creamy spots on the forewings and a row of 'eyes' along the hindwings. Mainly lives in woods, but now on the increase and often seen in gardens, especially those with hedgerows.

Common Blue
June to September, almost anywhere
Male is a small- to medium-sized, deep blue butterfly, noticeably larger than the holly blue. White edges to the wings. Female much browner, with hints of bluish above.

Holly Blue
April/May and July/September, England and Wales
A tiny blue butterfly, often seen fluttering high against a climbing shrub. Powder blue above, with black wing tips, and tiny black spots on pale blue below. Two broods, one in spring and the other in summer. Most likely blue butterfly to be found in gardens.

Other ways to attract butterflies

⚙ Put out windfall or rotten fruit – the juices will attract butter-flies, especially on warm, sunny days in autumn when red admirals are out and about.
⚙ Place a white or yellow sheet on the ground in the sunshine, or drape it over bramble bushes – this will often attract butter-flies, especially early in the day when they need to warm up.
⚙ Plant nectar-rich flowers such as honeysuckle, lavender and especially buddleia – also known as the 'butterfly bush'.
⚙ Go wild – a patch of stinging nettles in the corner of your garden is the ideal food plant for several different kinds of caterpillar.

Many people assume, wrongly, that the word 'butterfly' comes from 'flutterby'. In fact, the original 'butter-coloured fly' was the bright yellow brimstone.

Go moth-trapping

There can be few creatures as misunderstood as moths. Normally sensible people go into hysterical panic when they come across one; or think that just because the larvae of a couple of species destroy clothing, all moths must be harmful.

The truth is that Britain's 2,500 or so different kinds of moth are among our most varied, beautiful and fascinating creatures — and the good news is that they are surprisingly easy to see. All you need is a way to attract them so you can get a closer look …

There are all sorts of different ways to trap moths; some cheap and simple, others a bit more complicated and expensive. But whichever method you choose, you are guaranteed more or less instant success.

You can either attract them with light, or tempt them with food. Several trapping methods take advantage of moths' love of sweet, sugary substances, including alcohol.

One theory as to why moths are attracted by bright lights is that they use the moon to navigate, so that when a light is switched on they try to orient themselves in relation to it. But because the light is only a short distance away (as opposed to almost 400,000km between the Earth and the moon) the moth finds itself flying in ever decreasing circles until it hits the light. At this point its tiny brain assumes that the sun has come up, so it settles down to rest in the bottom of the trap.

When to trap moths

- Moths are out and about virtually all year round, but the largest numbers and greatest range of species are on the wing in late spring, summer and early autumn — and especially the months of June, July and August.
- Weather conditions play an important part: the best times for mothing are warm, humid nights with plenty of cloud cover and little or no wind. Although heavy rain will dampen their enthusiasm (and probably yours too), a spot of light drizzle can encourage more moths.

○ Finally, don't bother using light traps on moonlit nights, especially when there is a full moon, as they will be pretty ineffective.

How to do it

○ Dusking: the simplest and quickest way to find moths is simply to search for them using a bright torch and a butterfly net. The best places to look are nectar-rich plants where the moths will be feeding. Take a few small plastic containers with you to keep the moths in so you can get a good look at them later. Dusking works particularly well in the early evening when it is still light enough for you to see where you're going. It is also best early in the season – late winter to spring.

○ Sheeting: similar to dusking, but done by shining a powerful torch on to an old white sheet. Within a minute or two the moths will start to arrive, and you can either examine them as they rest on the sheet or put them into the plastic containers for a closer look later.

○ Sugaring: in a large saucepan, mix up about 250ml of dark beer (a stout or porter works best), a tin (roughly 500g) of black treacle and 1kg of dark brown (molasses or muscovado) sugar. Bring to the boil, simmer for a few minutes (adding a shot or two of rum if you wish), then take the pan off the heat and let it cool. Once the mixture is cold, transfer it into an old tin and use a paintbrush to smear it on to tree trunks, gateposts or pieces of wood. Do remember that this will stain so don't paint it on your garden fence! Sugaring tends to work best early on in the night when most moths are active.

○ Wine-roping: you use a similar recipe, but with red wine instead of beer; then soak lengths of rope in the mixture and hang them up from the branches of trees.

○ Outdoor lighting: many moths flutter to security and porch lights, so just switch them on and see what comes!

But if you're really keen on moth-trapping, and don't mind spending £200 or so (less if you share it among a group of you), then the best method is to use a full-scale 'Robinson trap' or 'Skinner trap', the latter named after an early pioneer of moth identification, Bernard Skinner.

These use a mercury vapour (MV) light bulb, which gives out a very bright beam of ultraviolet light which attracts the moths. You'll need a long extension cable as this will need to be plugged in at the mains. Don't look directly at the light as it can damage your eyesight.

The moment you turn on the light, the bulb will begin to warm up, and within a few minutes the moths will start to arrive. Once they reach the light source they slip down the Perspex sides into the bottom of the trap. Here they find cardboard egg boxes where they can settle down unharmed until you come and inspect the trap, either later that night or early the next morning.

When you inspect your trap, be careful as you remove the moths not to harm their wings. You'll need a good moth identification guide (details on page 267), and a notebook to write down details of what you find. It's also a good idea to bring a digital camera to take pictures of the moths you catch, so you can identify them at leisure later on.

Once you've removed and inspected the moths, make sure you release them somewhere with plenty of vegetation to hide behind. And don't put them all in one place as this will attract hungry birds.

If you live in a built-up area, make sure your bulb isn't visible from your neighbours' bedrooms, or the bright light may keep them up all night!

Moths have some of the most bizarre and delightful names of any of our wild creatures, including: Kentish glory, Chinese character, ghost moth, drinker, steamer, spinach, spruce carpet, bleached pug, belted beauty, swallow prominent, gothic, Blair's shoulder-knot, scarce merveille du jour, double kidney, Brighton wainscot, burnished brass, exile and, my favourite, setaceous Hebrew character.

Watch damselflies and dragonflies

Dragonflies, and their close relatives the damselflies, are among the fastest, largest, most brightly coloured and all-round impressive insects on Earth. Here are just a few amazing facts about them.

- Dragonflies have been around for over 300 million years — well before dinosaurs appeared.
- They can fly at speeds of almost 50km per hour.
- Their eyes have up to 30,000 different lenses.
- They are the tigers of the insect world: lone hunters, seizing, dispatching and devouring their prey with ruthless efficiency.
- Despite their fearsome reputation, they do not normally bite human beings, and cannot sting us either, but do predate on other flying insects.
- Although they live for up to seven years, they spend almost all that time underwater in larval form; adult dragonflies stay on the wing for just a few weeks.
- With a length of about 8cm, and a wingspan of 12cm, the emperor dragonfly is one of our largest insects.

There are about forty different kinds of dragonfly and damselfly in Britain. Damselflies are generally smaller, but the best way to tell the difference is the way they sit when perched.

Dragonflies stick their wings out from their body, looking a bit like a First World War biplane (except the pairs of wings are one in front of the other rather than top and bottom). The smaller, more match-like damselflies perch with their wings held along the length of their body, giving them a more streamlined appearance.

Different species appear at different times of year, with the earliest emerging on bright, sunny days in April, and the latest hanging around into the autumn. June, July and August are the ideal months; and warm, dry days the best kind of weather — dragonflies are unable to fly when it's raining or too cold.

In flight it can be quite hard to see their colours, but as soon as a dragonfly or damselfly comes in to land it reveals its beauty. Different species can be identified by the colours and patterns of

How to identify …
dragonflies
and damselflies

These stunning creatures can sometimes be quite challenging to identify, but using a combination of clues you should be able to work most of them out. Useful clues are:

- Shape: if it holds its wings out when perched, it's a dragonfly; if it folds them along the length of its body, it's a damselfly.
- Location: check out if the insect you think you're watching lives in this particular part of the country.
- Habitat: some dragonflies prefer specialist habitats such as heathland; others can be found anywhere with water — or even some distance away.
- Timing: different dragonflies come out at different times of year — again, check this out in a field guide.
- Size: sometimes hard to judge, but with practice you'll know if you're looking at a large hawker or a smaller darter; skimmers and chasers are somewhere in between.
- Colour and pattern: pay special attention to the head and thorax (chunky part of the body), the abdomen (the long part of the body) and the wings; also look for spots (or no spots!) on the wings.
- Habits: some dragonflies are brash and bold, flying over to check you out; others are shy and wary. Some fly almost constantly; others prefer to bask in the sunshine on a leaf or path.

How to identify ...
dragonflies and damselflies

Emperor
Our largest dragonfly and one of our largest insects. Males are blue on the abdomen and green on the head and thorax; females mainly green. Found in southern Britain from June to August.

Southern Hawker
Another huge dragonfly: mainly green and brown but with blue near the end of the abdomen. Found in England, Wales and lowland Scotland from July to September. Often flies right up to you to take a close look.

Brown Hawker
The only large dragonfly with yellowish-brown wings, and a brown body with odd spots of blue. Found in southern Britain, and one of the latest to appear, from August to October.

Migrant and Common Hawkers
Two very similar medium-to-large dragonflies: brown with blue and yellow markings. Common found more in the north, migrant in the south, from July to October.

Hairy Dragonfly

Mainly brown with blue and green markings. By far the earliest large dragonfly to appear, from late April to June, mostly in the south and east.

Four-spotted Chaser

A medium-sized, chunky dragonfly with two spots on each wing (making eight in all). Males mainly brown, females more yellow orange. Found throughout Britain from May to July.

Banded Demoiselle

A large damselfly, with delicately barred wings and a slender blue (male) or green (female) abdomen. Appears in large numbers in southern Britain from May to August.

Broad-bodied Chaser

Another chunky, medium-sized dragonfly – males are powder blue on the abdomen, females yellowish brown. Found in southern Britain from June to July.

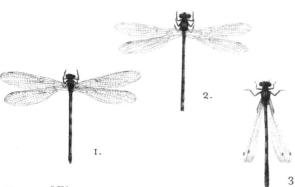

Common Darter

Small dragonfly; males are reddish brown, females yellow; spots on wings. Found across most of Britain from July to October – sometimes even later in the warmer south.

Damselflies

Several species of damselfly emerge on sunny days from late April through to August, including:

1. Common Blue, Azure and Variable: patterned bright blue and black and very hard to tell apart.
2. Blue-tailed: dark abdomen with a bright blue tip.
3. Large Red: reddish abdomen with black markings.
4. Red-eyed: dark abdomen with a blue tip and large red eyes.

their head, thorax (the chunky area behind the head from which the wings stick out) and the long abdomen.

As soon as they emerge, these insects are in a race against time to find a partner and breed, so that the female can lay the next generation of eggs beneath the surface of the water. Look out for two dragonflies or damselflies in a circular embrace as they mate.

Once the female has deposited her precious eggs, her parental duties are over: the eggs eventually hatch into tiny larvae, which feed voraciously under water for several years.

During this period they shed their skin several times as they grow, before metamorphosing into the adult and emerging into the open air via a plant stem.

Tips

❂ Make sure your binoculars are able to focus at least as close as three metres (preferably even closer), which will allow you to get fabulous views of perched dragonflies and damselflies without disturbing them.
❂ A good way to work out which species you're looking at is to take digital photos, then look them up in an identification guide when you get home.

Dragonflies and damselflies have all sorts of folk names, many of them referring to their supposed ability to bite or sting, including horse stinger, adderbolt and the devil's darning needle.

Give bumblebees a helping hand

It's sometimes said that it is scientifically impossible for a bumblebee to fly. Yet the bumblebee, seemingly unaware of this scientific 'fact', manages to fly anyway.

And thank goodness it does. For without pollination carried out by the humble bumblebee, about one-third of all the food in this country would never be able to grow. Many of our wild-flower meadows would never bloom. And our economy would lose out to the tune of about £1 billion a year.

Other reasons to welcome bumble-bees is that they are so beautiful — with their combinations of yellow, orange, black and white — and endangered, with half our British species on the critical list. So anything we can do to give our bumblebees a helping hand must be worthwhile.

Things to do

- Plant nectar-rich flowers — especially native species — in your garden; the more you plant, the more bumblebees you will attract — and the better they will pollinate your garden plants.
- Make sure you have flowers in bloom throughout the year — bumblebees will often emerge on sunny days in winter to stock up on nectar.
- Stop using pesticides — they are just as harmful to friendly creatures like bumblebees as they are to less welcome ones.
- Don't panic if a bumblebee comes close — many don't have a sting at all and even those that do are very unlikely to sting you.
- Put some bumblebee boxes in your flower beds — these are just like bird nest boxes but with two chambers, one for the queen and the other for the workers.
- Let part of your garden grow wild, with longer grass and scrub where the bumblebees may also nest.
- Log piles are also great places for bumblebees.
- Finally, if you come across a hibernating bumblebee in your garden shed, try not to disturb it — emerging too early or in cold, wet weather may be fatal.

Making a home for solitary bees

Here is a simple way to do this from the conservation organisation Buglife.

- ۞ Cut bamboo cane (internal diameter up to about 1cm) into sections about 10-20cm long (making sure you cut between the nodes along each cane).
- ۞ Bundle them up using garden twine or string.
- ۞ Hang them up in a garden shed or garage — ideally in a place where they get some sunshine during the course of the day. Don't put them anywhere that they might get exposed to rain.
- ۞ Wait and see what comes … As well as solitary bees you may also attract different species of wasp, whose larva will feed on the bee grubs.

The myth that bumblebees can't fly goes back to the 1930s, when an aeronautics engineer used a combination of the creature's size, weight and wing length to work out that it could not possibly get airborne. What he overlooked was how the bumblebee flaps its wings — not up and down, like a bird, but in a complex figure of eight — which when carried out two hundred times a second enables the bee to fly.

Take a really close look at an ant colony

Go to the ant, thou sluggard; consider her ways, and be wise.
PROVERBS, 6:6

What wonderful creatures ants are. Among the strongest (weight for weight), most intelligent and sociable insects on Earth, they are endlessly fascinating to observe and study.

Ants live in underground colonies: a series of interconnected chambers, tunnels and passageways with separate areas for storing

How to identify ...
ladybirds and other bugs

Ladybird, ladybird, fly away home
Your house is on fire and your children are gone
All except one, and that's Little Anne
For she has crept under the warming pan.

Ladybirds are among our most attractive and best-known insects;
and unlike most creepy-crawlies are generally liked by people —
apart from when the occasional 'summer plague' of these little
insects hits the headlines.

The name 'ladybird' refers to the Virgin Mary (known as 'Our
Lady'), and was given to these tiny beetles because they mainly eat
pests such as aphids, and so have always been popular with farmers and gardeners.

Their bright colours — reds, oranges and yellows — are in fact a
warning sign to predators such as birds not to eat them because
they taste nasty. To make themselves even nastier, ladybirds
secrete a foul-smelling liquid from their knee joints — which will
stain your hands if you are not careful.

Ladybirds are in fact beetles — and make up just 1 per cent of
our 4,000 beetle species. Many of these are rare and obscure,
and don't even have a common English name — the exceptions
are some of our best-known insects, such as the cockchafer,
glow-worm and stag beetle. Most of these species emerge for a
brief life on the wing from May through to August — taking
advantage of the warm summer months — before mating, laying
their eggs and then dying.

How to identify ...
ladybirds and other bugs

black on yellow

yellow on black

2-spot Ladybird
One of our commonest ladybirds, and easily recognised by the pattern of two black spots on an orange background. Found all over Britain from March to October.

7-spot Ladybird
Another very common and widespread ladybird, found throughout Britain in the spring and summer months. Like other ladybirds, often found indoors in autumn and winter, when they hibernate in clusters. Count the spots to identify.

14-spot Ladybird
Having so many black spots gives this ladybird a very different appearance: lots of black on a yellowish-orange background. Mainly found in southern Britain from April to September.

Harlequin Ladybird
This beefy invader is a new arrival, coming in on plants from abroad via garden centres. Very variable in colour and appearance — including yellowish orange, through red to black, and with anything between twenty-one spots and none at all — but is larger than most common British ladybirds. The commonest forms are orange with lots of black spots, or black with two or four spots. Now the commonest ladybird in parts of southern Britain, and heading northwards.

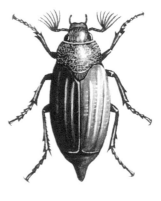

Stag Beetle

Our largest land beetle, and a truly magnificent beast. Males have huge antlers, which they use to fight each other in order to win the females. Larvae spend years hidden in rotting wood, before emerging for their one brief shining moment for a few weeks every summer. Often seen on warm evenings in June and July, especially in south east England.

Cockchafer

Also known as the May bug because of the time it appears, this large, bulky beetle flies around at dusk, sometimes bumping into people as it does so. Brown and shiny, oval in shape, with a pointed tip to the abdomen.

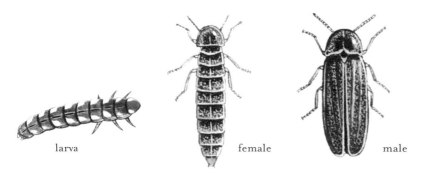

larva   female   male

Glow-worm

Not a worm, but a beetle – and a rather peculiar one. The wingless female is able to shine a bright green light to attract her flying mate. Look for glow-worms after dark on warm summer nights – grassy verges and woodland rides are the best places. Commonest in southern Britain.

Rose Chafer

A shiny, green version of the cockchafer which generally appears from May to September, feeding on flowers.

food and looking after the eggs and young. These are created and maintained by thousands of 'worker ants', wingless females, every one of which is at the service of the queen – the colony's pampered egg-laying machine.

You can watch ant colonies on a sunny day, as the workers emerge and scatter in search of food to bring back underground.

Try catching a few ants in a plastic container and taking a close look through a magnifying glass. Notice that like all insects their bodies are divided into three parts: the head, thorax and abdomen; with two antennae attached to the head and six legs emerging from the thorax.

Another way to get an insight into the lives of ants is to create your own colony, known as a 'formicarium' or 'ant farm'. This allows you to see the tunnels and cavities created by the worker ants. You can either make your own – with two sheets of glass or Perspex sandwiched close together and filled with sand or soil – or buy one by mail order or online.

One introduced species of ant from Argentina has formed a 'supercolony', which stretches more than 6,000 kilometres from northern Italy, via the south of France, to Spain. The total number of individual ants in the colony runs into the billions.

Make a home for minibeasts

When I was growing up we called them 'creepy-crawlies' or 'bugs'. Nowadays we use the term 'minibeasts' to cover the thousands of insects and other invertebrates that we come across in our daily lives. These include true insects – such as flies, bees and wasps, butterflies and moths (and their caterpillars) and various beetles and bugs – as well as other, unrelated groups – like spiders, snails and slugs.

The best way to get to know minibeasts is to keep them yourself. By watching them grow and develop, and seeing how they change at different times in their life-cycle, you will really begin to appreciate these tiny creatures.

What you need

◎ A tank: made from glass or Perspex, roughly 30–75cm long, 30–50cm wide and 30–50cm deep – with a secure, tight-fitting lid. You can buy tanks from your local pet shop or by mail order from Internet suppliers.
◎ The filling: the best kind is peat soil from a garden centre – *never* use compost as this contains chemicals which will be harmful to the minibeasts.
◎ Extras: old leaves and rotted wood; dry twigs and small branches; old flowerpots.
◎ Water: a small plastic dish or old jam-jar lid; and a small spray device sold by garden centres to water house plants.
◎ Food: bits of fruit and vegetables.

What to do

Fill the bottom of your tank with soil, to a depth of about 10–15 cm, and spray it with water to make it damp. Then arrange the twigs, branches and leaves around the tank so the minibeasts have got plenty of places where they can hide or sit. You can also use bits of bark, stones or old flowerpots to make hidey-holes. Sink the jam-jar lid or plastic dish into the soil and fill with water, then spray again to create a nice, humid atmosphere.

It's now time to introduce your minibeasts. Avoid putting in carnivorous creatures (such as spiders, ladybirds, centipedes and some kinds of beetle) as they will eat all the others. The best creatures to keep are slugs, snails, woodlice and millipedes, as they should be able to live happily alongside each other.

You'll also need to provide food: bits of fruit and vegetables are ideal – cut them up into small chunks to make it easier for the minibeasts to carry.

Tips

- Keep your tank somewhere warm, but not too hot as it may dry out.
- Make sure you give your minibeasts a sense of the daily cycle by switching off lights at night.
- Remove any uneaten food before it goes mouldy.
- After handling minibeasts or the filling in the tank, always wash your hands.
- If you go on holiday get someone else to feed your minibeasts and keep the tank clean.

At least two out of every three species on the planet are minibeasts — of which almost 50,000 different kinds occur in Britain.

Lie down in long grass and stare at the sky

I long for scenes where man has never trod,
A place where woman never smiled or wept;
There to abide with my Creator, God,
And sleep as I in childhood sweetly slept:
Untroubling and untroubled where I lie,
The grass below — above, the vaulted sky.

JOHN CLARE

For many of us, one of our first childhood memories is the sensation of lying down in long grass and staring up at a clear blue sky, as time seemed to stand still.

So why not do it again …? It really is a wonderful way to relax and shed the cares of this world.

Become a bat detective

There are seventeen different kinds of bat in Britain — over one-quarter of all our mammal species — yet apart from the occasional glimpse at dusk on a warm summer's evening, we hardly ever see them. That's because they spend the daylight hours roosting in the attics of houses, old barns or caves, and only emerge at night to hunt for their insect prey.

Some people are put off by all the folklore about bats, so let's get a few things straight. Apart from South American vampire bats, they don't suck blood; they don't get tangled in your hair; and bats are most certainly not blind. In fact they have pretty good eyesight, although they track down their prey using a very different technique.

Bats hunt by 'echo-location' — uttering a series of rapid clicks which 'bounce off' any objects in the air. By listening to the echo made when the sound hits the object, the bat knows how close it is, even if it can't actually see it.

Bats also know whether what they are hearing is made by a solid object like a wall, or a moving prey item like a moth – enabling them either to avoid a collision or to catch their dinner.

If you want to learn more about bats, the best way is to go on an organised bat walk. These usually take place at dusk during the spring and summer, and are run by local bat groups and wildlife trusts.

Because bats call at very high frequencies – generally too high for the human ear to detect – the group leader will usually bring a 'bat detector'. This clever instrument can convert the calls into a series of clicks which we are then able to hear.

Different kinds of bats call at different sound frequencies; some bats have very rhythmic calls, and others warble, almost like a bird. So an experienced 'bat-man' or 'bat-woman' will be able to identify the particular species you are hearing.

On some bat walks, especially later in the year, the leader may look inside bat nesting boxes and bring out a bat for you to look at. You'll be amazed at how tiny they are, with such delicate wings – yet the bat is a really impressive flyer, rivalling even the birds with its aerobatic skills.

The smallest British bats, the pipistrelles, are about three centimetres long and weigh as little as four grams – about the same as a two-pence coin. The largest, the noctule, has a wingspan of 30–40 centimetres and weighs about 25–40 grams – about the same as a house sparrow.

Collect birds' feathers

Quite rightly, collecting birds' eggs is against the law. But it's fine to make a collection of feathers – and a great way to learn just what complex structures they are.

For its weight, a feather is one of the strongest objects in the natural world: capable of carrying its owner on journeys of many thousands of miles.

Feathers are made from a substance known as keratin — the same as that found in human hair and nails. It is strong and incredibly light, as well as flexible enough to withstand the stresses and strains of a bird's aerial existence.

Their structure is a miracle of evolution: a hollow shaft down the centre supports hundreds of delicate filaments, known as 'barbs', along each side. These mesh together using even tinier filaments known as 'barbules', creating a tight and highly effective tool for flight.

Most of the feathers you will find are the larger wing feathers, known as 'primaries'. Because these get so much wear and tear, birds shed them regularly (usually once a year) in a process known as moult. The easiest ones to find are from larger birds such as crows (all black), pigeons (three bars of different shades of grey) and gulls (grey with black and white on the tip). Park ponds and riverbanks are a good place to look for feathers from ducks, geese and swans.

To examine a feather's structure, run your finger along one of the barbs and see how they come apart, then fit back together — just like the two sides of a zip. You can also use a magnifying glass to see the individual barbs and barbules. Once you've had a good look, use a pair of scissors to cut open the shaft — revealing its hollow, air-filled inside.

Making an old-fashioned quill pen

You can use larger feathers to make an old-fashioned quill pen.

- Start by dipping the tip of the feather in boiling water to soften it.
- Then use a sharp penknife to make a neat, horizontal cut across the end of the feather; then make two diagonal cuts to create a triangular-shaped nib.
- Finally make a neat cut about 10mm in length from the tip of the nib back up the handle, and a cut across the tip of the nib.
- Carefully dip your quill into a bottle of ink, allowing the ink to rise up the shaft of the quill.

❂ Then start to write. This will take practice at first, as quill pens are rather messy — but with a bit of effort you'll soon master the art.

Different birds have a very different number of feathers — smaller birds, such as robins, have fewer than 5,000; while larger birds, such as swans, may have more than 25,000 feathers.

Go badger-watching

The badger is one of our largest and most impressive land mammals. Fully-grown adults can weigh as much as 12kg, about the same as a three-year-old child.

Badgers are shy animals, very wary of humans — and with good reason, as they have often been persecuted in the past, and in some places still are. But they are commoner than you might think, and with expert help can be surprisingly easy to see.

When to watch

Despite what many people think, badgers don't actually hibernate; but they are far less active during the autumn and winter months, and tend to do their foraging under cover of darkness during the long winter nights.

So the months from May to August give the best chance to see them — the cubs are more active and the animals are more likely to be seen in daylight.

Where to watch

Badgers are found over much of Britain, though are missing from parts of eastern England and the Scottish Highlands. They are more common towards the damper south and west – where the soil is moist enough for them to dig easily for their favourite food of earthworms.

Badgers live in a network of interconnected tunnels known as a sett. The same sett may have been used by local badgers for decades – even centuries – something reflected in local place names such as Brockenhurst in Hampshire ('brock' is an old name for the badger).

Badger setts are sometimes hard to find, and you risk disturbing the animals if you don't really know what you're looking for, so it's best to go on an organised badger-watching outing. These are run by county Wildlife Trusts and local badger groups, and are advertised on the Internet or at your local library. Most run from April/May to September/October to coincide with peak badger activity.

Tips

- Be in the right place. The badger's sense of smell is extremely sensitive, so make sure you stand downwind from the sett (so you have the wind on your face when you're looking towards it).
- Be still. Although badgers don't have very good eyesight they will notice sudden movements – so wear dull shades of clothing and keep as still as you can.
- Be quiet. Badgers are very sensitive to noise, so wear clothing that doesn't rustle, don't talk loudly as you approach the sett or while you're waiting, and watch where you walk – a cracking twig may send the badger straight back underground. And once you've finished watching and you're walking home, don't talk loudly – that will disturb the badgers you've just been observing.

Spend the night in a tent in your garden

When I was about eight or nine I played a trick on my mother, which enabled me and my friend Alan to spend the night in a tent in his garden. We simply told her that Alan's parents had given us permission to camp out for the night, and asked if she would say yes too. Before she thought of phoning them to confirm, we cycled as fast as we could round to Alan's house and told his mum and dad the same thing. By the time they spoke, each assumed the other had approved our nocturnal adventure, so we were allowed to go ahead!

Even the most familiar place can seem strange and mysterious when experienced at night – and nowhere more so than your own back garden. So choose a fine, warm summer night, pitch your tent with plenty of time to spare, and get everything you need for a night's adventure.

- Sleeping bags to keep you warm.
- Blow-up mattresses or something soft to lie on.
- A torch or bike light, plus a spare.
- Food and drink for a midnight snack.

One of the nicest things about sleeping out in your garden is that you'll probably be woken up by the sound of the dawn chorus. Open the flaps of your tent and just enjoy the sensation of hearing this wonderful orchestra of birdsong from the comfort of your bed.

Make a compost heap

My mother was a keen gardener, and like anyone brought up during the Second World War had an almost fanatical loathing of waste. So any grass cuttings, vegetable peelings or dead leaves would be taken in a wheelbarrow down to the end of the garden, and flung on to the compost heap. Little did I realise then that this smelly pile of rotting vegetation might be home to two of our most exciting reptiles: the slow-worm and the grass snake. If I had, I might have dared to take a closer look.

Wildlife just loves compost heaps — their equivalent of a centrally heated home with a top-of-the-range kitchen. It's not just reptiles that are attracted by the warmth generated by all that decomposing compost: slugs, snails and other minibeasts all make their home there, sometimes attracting birds to feed on them. And our favourite garden animal, the hedgehog, often seeks shelter there.

And compost heaps are a more environmentally friendly way of providing compost for your garden — much better to use recycled leftovers than to buy peat-based composts whose production causes harm to the environment. Every home should have one.

What kind of compost heap should I have?

You have three basic choices.

- The loose heap: simply a pile in one corner of your garden — easy for animals to get in and out of but not so efficient at generating heat.
- The boxed heap: easily constructed with bits of wood and chicken wire — more efficient though less accessible.
- The fancy composter: these can be bought from garden centres or by mail order, and have a range of different chambers so that you can get easy access to compost at different stages of its rotting process.

Where to put your compost heap

A hidden corner of your garden is best as it will be out of the way – but avoid too shady a spot as compost needs some sunshine to stop it getting waterlogged. The area should also be reasonably level so that your heap will be stable.

What you need to make a boxed heap

- Four wooden fence posts – 10cm x 10cm across and approximately 1.25–1.5 metres long.
- Wooden planks or chicken wire to make the sides.
- Straw or small twigs for drainage.
- A heavy-duty mallet.
- Nails or tacks.
- A layer of carpet, tarpaulin or heavy-duty polythene.

How to make the heap

- Start by hammering the four fence posts firmly into the ground.
- Next, either nail the planks to the posts, or tack the chicken wire around them – but make sure one side is easy to open, allowing you to remove the compost when it's ready to use.
- Line the bottom of the box with the straw or twigs.
- Then start off the process by adding your garden waste in layers about 15–20cm thick, alternating grass cuttings, leaves and so on with a thin layer of soil in between.
- Add water if the material is too dry.
- Finally, when the layers have reached the top, cover with the piece of carpet, tarpaulin or polythene and make the lid secure.
- Wait about three months while the compost 'cooks', then open your front hatch to remove it for use.

THINGS YOU CAN PUT IN	THINGS TO AVOID
fallen leaves	garden chemicals
vegetable and fruit peelings	dog or cat waste
shredded paper	any meat product
used tea bags	thick woody stems or twigs
weeds	anything man-made
hedge clippings	leftover food
grass cuttings	anything that might grow —
dead leaves	seedheads, roots, etc.

The ideal internal temperature of your compost heap should range from 48 to 65°C, though temperatures can rise as high as 70° — warm enough to heat up a mug of tea or cook an egg.

Go on a city safari

Cities are often known as 'urban jungles' — and you might think that this would mean wild creatures would struggle to find a home there. But far from being tough, hostile environments for wildlife, they in fact provide everything the creature-about-town needs.

Whether a wild creature is looking for food, water, shelter, light or heat, the modern city provides it. As a result, a whole host of animals — and plants — have moved lock, stock and barrel into our urban areas.

They're not just surviving there, but thriving. Every single major animal group — from birds of prey to deer, and from seabirds to seals — can be found in at least one British city. And because these animals have got used to living alongside millions of us, they are often far less wary than their country cousins.

Take the urban fox. In the countryside, where until recently they have been hunted, foxes are shy creatures, rarely seen apart from a bushy red tail disappearing out of sight. Yet in our towns and cities they will stroll down the street without a care in the world – knowing that as long as they can avoid the traffic, they are safe.

One of the best ways to get to know the wildlife of a town or city is to treat it just like any other place to watch wildlife – and go on an urban safari. By planning your route so it takes in a range of different locations and habitats, you should not only see a wide range of plants and animals, but get great views as well.

Tips

- Get hold of a really detailed map – the Ordnance Survey Pathfinder range (1:25,000 scale or 4cm to 1km) is ideal.
- Plan your route – try to include a patch of woodland, the local park, a river or canal – as each new habitat is likely to bring new sightings.
- Take a pair of binoculars, a couple of field guides and a notebook to write down what you see.
- As always, a digital camera is a good way to record sightings (especially plants and insects) for you to identify later, when you get home.
- Don't forget to look down – cities, and especially ports like London, Liverpool and Bristol, have all sorts of exotic foreign plants growing in some unlikely places.

Classic city locations and what to look for

- London: red and fallow deer and ring-necked parakeets in Richmond Park; stag beetles on Wimbledon Common; peregrines on Tate Modern; cormorants, herons and swans on the Thames; water voles, bats and birdlife at the London Wetland Centre.
- Birmingham: kingfishers on the canal network.
- Glasgow: foxes in the suburbs of the West End.

- Brighton: huge winter roost of starlings on the Palace Pier.
- Dundee: red squirrels in the city parks.
- Newcastle: nesting kittiwakes on the Tyne Bridge; seals and the occasional otter in the Tyne.
- Bristol: peregrines and buzzards over Avon Gorge.
- Manchester: peregrines on the Arndale Shopping centre.
- Cardiff: salmon leaping on the River Taff.

Native to India, the origin of the flocks of bright green parakeets now living in London's parks and gardens is the subject of much speculation. Some people believe they escaped from a film studio at Shepperton; others think they got free when a container broke open at Heathrow Airport. But the most intriguing suggestion is that a pair of parakeets, named Adam and Eve, was released by rock star Jimi Hendrix from his Carnaby Street flat in 1969 — the very year the birds were first seen in the wild in Britain.

Look for snakes and lizards

Of the 8,000 or so different kinds of reptile found in the world, just six are native to the British Isles: three kinds of lizard and three snakes. They are the common lizard, sand lizard, slow-worm (which despite its name and appearance is a legless lizard), grass snake, smooth snake and adder (the only British reptile poisonous to human beings).

This sextet of reptiles can be found in a range of habitats and regions, although most prefer dry, sandy soils and are commoner in the warmer south than the cooler north. That's because snakes and lizards are cold-blooded, so they need warm, sunny conditions in order to heat up their bodies and become active.

Two species — the smooth snake and the sand lizard — are quite scarce, and mainly found on the dry heaths of Dorset, Hampshire and Surrey. The other four are found throughout much of lowland Britain, though the common lizard is the only reptile found in Ireland.

Tips for finding snakes and lizards

- Go to the right location: snakes and lizards are quite fussy about where they live. Grass snakes like damp, grassy areas such as the banks of rivers and canals; slow-worms love compost heaps; while adders and common lizards (and the rarer smooth snake and sand lizard) prefer dry, sandy heaths.
- Go at the right time of year: all six British reptiles hibernate during the autumn and winter, usually hiding away in September or October and emerging again the following March or April. The best times to look for them are on fine days in April and May, and again late in the season just before they go into hiding.
- Go during the right weather: warm, sunny days are ideal, because snakes and lizards emerge to soak up the sun's rays and warm their bodies. But you can also try looking just after a shower or longer spell of rain: when the sun comes out, so will the reptiles.

How to identify ...
snakes and lizards

Britain is not exactly blessed with reptiles – in fact, we only have
six species in all. Yet these can still be pretty tricky to identify,
especially as you may only get a fleeting glimpse of your quarry as
it slithers or scampers away into the undergrowth ...

How to identify ...
snakes and lizards

Grass Snake

Our commonest and most widespread snake, usually found in damp areas near water, and frequently seen swimming. Greenish olive, with darker blotches along the sides; but most obvious feature is the bright yellow collar.

Adder

Britain's only venomous animal, but far more likely to slither away than bite you. Its thickset, chunky body and distinctive diamond-shaped markings make it fairly easy to identify. Usually found on sandy heaths or moors; also on the edge of woodland. Often basks in the sun, especially in early spring.

Smooth Snake

This rare reptile lives on the sandy heaths and commons of southern England, where it may be seen alongside the superficially similar adder. Generally less well marked than the adder, more slender and grey brown in colour.

Slow-worm

Much smaller and more slender than all the snakes, and a lighter, golden brown colour. Has a more streamlined appearance, with the head and neck appearing as an extension of the body rather than showing a bulge. Often found in gardens, especially compost heaps.

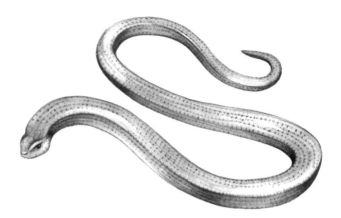

Common Lizard

Usually grey brown, with dark markings along its sides and back. Some males can appear quite green, so beware confusion with the rarer sand lizard. Found in a range of habitats throughout Britain, usually on grassy areas, moors and heaths.

Sand Lizard

Our rarest lizard is also our most beautiful: males are bright emerald green, especially during the breeding season, while females are paler brown with dark markings along their sides. Looks larger and more thickset than the common lizard. Apart from one outpost in Lancashire, found only on our southern heaths.

○ Go at the right time of day: as the sun rises in the sky and heats up the ground, snakes and lizards begin to emerge from their hiding places. This is often the best time of day to find them, as they bask in the sun to warm up. Later on, as the sun's heat gets stronger, they are harder to find, as they no longer need to stay out in the open to keep warm. Late afternoon to early evening is also a good time, as reptiles often sunbathe again as the temperature begins to drop.

○ Look in the right place: on heaths, seek out sunny areas on south-facing slopes, sheltered from the wind. Snakes and lizards will use these as suntraps, lying flat against the ground in order to make the most of the sun's warmth. Slow-worms and grass snakes often live in compost heaps, but make sure you don't disturb them when you're searching.

○ Look in the right way: walk slowly and steadily, as reptiles are very sensitive to movement. Keep the sun behind you, but watch your shadow, as this too will disturb a basking reptile.

○ Look for signs: snakes and lizards have to shed their skin from time to time, to enable them to grow, so you may find discarded skins — a sure sign that reptiles are in the area.

○ Listen: when a snake or lizard moves it rustles the vegetation — so if you hear something move, wait quietly for a few minutes to see if it comes out again.

It is often said that snakes were banished from Ireland by St Patrick. But the truth is that after the end of the last Ice Age, snakes were unable to reach Ireland before sea levels rose, and the land bridge from Scotland disappeared beneath the waters of the Irish Sea.

Naughty stuff

After my early attempts at making perfume out of rose petals, I graduated to more mischievous pastimes. Typical of boys of my generation (and quite a few girls, too), I loved making weapons out of anything I could find outdoors. Sometimes this simply involved picking the end off a plant and using it as a dart or pellet; other forms of attack were more complex and time-consuming — and all were great fun! Children are probably now discouraged from doing these things because of spurious health and safety fears — but here they are anyway.

Make itching powder from rose hips

Open up a rose hip, take a close look, and you'll see that the seeds are encased in tiny hairs. When put down the back of a schoolmate's shirt they cause an unpleasant itching — a trick used by generations of schoolchildren to liven up a dull lesson.

During the Second World War, when citrus fruits such as oranges and lemons were in short supply, scientists discovered that rose hips contained huge concentrations of vitamin C. As a result, several generations of children (until at least the 1960s, when I was growing up) enjoyed being given a daily dose of a sweet and tasty concoction called rose hip syrup.

Use seeds and grasses as darts and pellets

In late summer, all kinds of grasses produce seeds or seed heads that can be used as pellets or darts to throw at each other.

Among my favourites are:

- Wild barley: pull off the end to use as a highly effective dart — not only is it a straight and accurate flyer, it also sticks to woollen jumpers and fleeces.
- Plantain: the stems of the ribwort plantain can be wound around themselves to flick off the heads — creating a very satisfying pellet which can be aimed accurately at your opponent. The plant itself has gained several folk names as a result — including 'fighting cocks' and 'hard heads'.
- Burdock: the sticky seed heads of this common plant are ideal for throwing at unsuspecting friends, as they stick to almost anything.
- Grass whistle: this is a less antisocial game — simply pick a broad blade of grass, put it between your palms and blow — with practice you should be able to produce a range of satisfying (and sometimes rude) sounds.
- Cleavers: this annual plant spreads its seeds via a fruit with hooked barbs which attach to any animal passing by — including us. They make a splendid missile, as, like the burdock, they stick to almost anything. Among the folk names for cleavers are beggar's lice, everlasting friendship, stick-a-back and, my favourite, sticky-willy.

plantain

cleavers

Burdock is so sticky it inspired the inventor of Velcro — the product used in many modern items of clothing as an alternative to zips or buttons. According to the book Flora Britannica, *some children now call burdock 'the Velcro plant'.*

burdock

wild barley

Make a peashooter out of an elder stem

This idea comes from my father-in-law Mike, who was evacuated from London to Barnstaple during the Second World War, and has many happy memories of bunking off school to play in the fields and lanes of the North Devon countryside. He used the stems of cow parsley, the fluffy white plant that grows along the verges of country lanes from May onwards, but you get an even better peashooter using the harder stems of an elder.

Using a sharp penknife, cut a section about 20cm long from the straightest stem you can find, to create a long, straight, hollow tube about twice the thickness of a pen.

Put a few dried peas (the small round ones are the best) in the base of the tube; put your lips to the tube, and blow as hard as you can.

Things to do with flowers

Wild flowers are amongst our most beautiful natural objects, bringing a splash of colour to all sorts of places, from roadside verges to hedgerows, and woodland clearings to building sites. Our grandparents' generation used them for dozens of things: here are just a few.

Pick a bunch of wild flowers and press them

In Victorian times, every young lady — and many young men — would eagerly await the spring and summer months, when they could pick bunches of wild flowers and present them to their intended as a token of their undying love.

But cut flowers would only last a few days, so one way to keep them for longer was to press them. Flower pressing was especially popular among the upper classes, and Queen Victoria herself enjoyed the pastime.

The tradition of drying wild flowers to preserve them goes back much longer than this: examples have been found in ancient Egyptian tombs and Renaissance Bibles.

But although pressed flowers are still often used by artists and craftspeople, most children (and indeed quite a few adults) have never enjoyed this simple pleasure. And why? Mainly because conservationists keep banging on about how terrible it is to pick wild flowers there is even the possibility that the European Union will pass a law making the picking of wild flowers punishable by a jail sentence or a hefty fine …

To which I say … *nonsense*! If you are going to learn about nature, you need to get real, hands-on experience. And while digging up wild flowers to grow in your garden should not be en-

couraged, picking a few blooms to take home really isn't going to do any harm. So once you've gathered your favourite flowers, why not press them to keep them looking almost as good as the day they were picked?

What you need

- A sealable plastic box to collect your specimens.
- A large, heavy book (old telephone directories are ideal).
- Some plain white paper.
- A heavy weight — either a couple of bricks, or a large plastic container you can fill with water and seal up.
- A flat piece of wood (or a tea tray) — to be placed between the weight and the book to make sure you press evenly.
- A pair of tweezers to handle the delicate pressed flowers without damaging them.
- Clear glue.
- Scissors.
- Adhesive plastic film to protect design.
- The flowers themselves: almost any small, simple bloom will do, such as buttercups, pansies, poppies, daisies, forget-me-nots — but not complex flowers such as daffodils.

Tip

Make sure the flowers are as fresh as possible. Ideally, press them as soon as you can after picking; but if you can't, store them in a plastic bag or box in the fridge. Don't add water as this will speed up the decaying process.

What to do next

- Arrange your flowers on a sheet of paper, with the flowers separated so they don't touch each other.

- Cover with a second sheet of paper, and put inside your large book, leaving at least 1cm of pages between each set of flowers.
- Place the flat piece of wood or tea tray on top of the book, and place the weights on top.
- After about a week, remove the weights and open the book carefully.
- Using the tweezers, delicately lift each flower off the paper, taking great care not to damage the petals.

Once you have enough specimens, you can make all sorts of lovely designs by arranging them on white or coloured card (pastel shades are best), then sticking them down using household glue (the type that dries clear).

To protect your finished design, you can cover with adhesive plastic film, then trim with scissors to the required size and shape; or use a portable laminator to seal them in plastic.

You can then turn your designs into simple greetings cards or bookmarks, or put them in photo frames as gifts — a nice memory of a summer's walk in the woods.

Make elderflower fritters and elderflower cordial

Every June, my mother and I would walk around the local hedgerows picking elderflowers, which she took home to make elderflower wine. The cloudy, yellow liquid always looked enticing, but when I tried some it tasted horrible! I don't know whether this was due to my undeveloped palate or the quality of the wine.

Depending on where you live in the country, elderflowers bloom between late May and early July. Try to pick them when they have just come into bloom as they will taste fresher — and have fewer insects on them.

How to identify …
meadow flowers

Hay meadows — and the wild flowers that grow there — were once a common sight throughout lowland Britain, livening up even the dullest summer day with a splash of colour. But since the end of the Second World War, modern farming methods have destroyed more than 95 per cent of hay meadows in our countryside — making some of these once-common plants very rare indeed. The good news is that local Wildlife Trusts have saved many of our remaining hay meadows, and hold regular open days so you can enjoy the same experience as your grandparents did when they were children.

How to identify ...
meadow flowers

Meadow Buttercup
The classic plant of grassy fields and meadows: tall, with buttery-yellow flowers growing on several stems on each plant.

Field Scabious
A tall plant usually found on chalky soils, with rounded purplish-blue flowers which appear from June into the autumn, growing on tall stalks.

Bird's-foot Trefoil
This member of the pea family has clusters of bright yellow flowers, streaked with red — it is also sometimes called the 'egg-and-bacon plant'. After flowering from June to September, produces the distinctive three-pronged seed pods resembling a bird's foot, giving the plant its name.

Ox-eye Daisy
Large, showy daisy with long, white petals in a cluster around the bright yellow centre. Grows along roadside verges as well as meadows, from May through to October.

Yellow Rattle
This annual plant is often found in meadows as it stops grass growing, so other flowering plants can do well. Tall, with serrated leaves, and yellow flowers appearing from June to September. After flowering, the seeds rattle inside their cases.

Lady's Bedstraw
This attractive plant with its large clusters of yellow flowers spreads across grassland so effectively it was once used to stuff mattresses — hence its name. The flowers appear from June to September.

Meadowsweet

Appears from June to August in wet meadows and ditches: sprays of fluffy, creamy-white flowers with a sweet smell.

Viper's Bugloss

The tall, blue flowers of viper's bugloss appear in meadows from May to September, often towering above the other wild flowers. Once thought to cure adder bites – hence its peculiar name.

Meadow Cranesbill

Tall, attractive perennial with cup-shaped bluish-purple flowers; appearing from June to September. Look inside the petals to see the pale white markings that guide bees down into the flower towards the nectar. Name comes from seed heads, which are long and narrow like a crane's bill.

Snake's-head Fritillary

One of our rarest, weirdest and most beautiful plants, this flower of wet meadows appears briefly for a few weeks from April into May: drooping, pinkish-purple flowers hanging from tall, slender stems. Now only found in a few colonies in central southern England.

Purple Loosestrife

One of our most striking plants of summer, its tall stems with their bunches of deep purple flowers appearing from June to September. Likes boggy ground, and often found in wet meadows or near open water.

Early Purple Orchid

As its name suggests, one of the first orchids to bloom, its tall, spiky purple flowers appearing from April to June. Leaves are glossy green, with dark blotches.

Rosebay Willowherb

Not strictly a meadow plant, but a common sight in summer on any disturbed ground, such as roadside verges or building sites in towns and cities. Tall stems with delicate sprays of pinkish-purple flowers.

And if you can, avoid picking flowers growing right next to a busy road as they may be polluted, or near farm fields where they may have been sprayed with chemicals.

Don't be put off by the flowers' rather odd smell — they have a wonderful flavour, as these two very different recipes show.

Elderflower fritters

INGREDIENTS
1 egg
50g plain flour
100ml milk
sunflower oil
5 elderflower heads — shaken to remove small insects but *not* washed, as this will remove the flavour
caster sugar to dip

METHOD
1. Separate the egg into white and yolk.
2. Mix the egg yolk, milk and flour together until smooth; put to one side for about 20 minutes.
3. Whisk the egg white until it begins to show 'peaks'; then fold gently into the batter mixture.
4. Heat 2–3cm of sunflower oil in a deep-sided pan until it is almost smoking.
5. Dip each elderflower head by the stem into the batter; then drop into the hot oil. Cook for 1–2 minutes until it starts to turn golden brown.
6. Take out of the oil and place head down on kitchen paper to drain off excess oil.
7. Dip into the caster sugar and serve while still piping hot.

Elderflower cordial

INGREDIENTS
20 elderflower heads
zest and juice of 4 oranges
zest and juice of 2 lemons
up to 2kg caster sugar
80g citric acid (available from your local chemist)
1.5 litres water

METHOD
1. Trim the flower heads, removing as much stalk as possible, shake to remove insects, then put them in a very large bowl or saucepan.
2. In a separate saucepan add the sugar and water. Bring to the boil and stir until the sugar has dissolved.
3. Pare the zest from the oranges and lemons and add to the bowl with the elderflowers. Juice the oranges and add this to the bowl, along with the lemons cut into slices.
4. Pour over the hot syrup, stirring to mix the flower heads and fruits, then stir in the citric acid. Cover with a clean cloth and leave at room temperature for 24 hours.
5. The next day, strain the liquid through a sieve lined with muslin and pour the cordial into clean bottles with screw tops, and store in the fridge. This can be used like a squash or cordial, diluted with about 6–10 parts water depending on your taste. It works especially well with sparkling water.

Bunches of elder leaves were often hung up inside homes, as their pungent smell acts as a natural fly repellent.

Blow dandelion clocks

All through the summer, as dandelion flowers turn into seeds, you can play a game with them. Break off the stalk carefully, making sure you don't shake it as the seeds will fall off before you are ready. Then blow the seeds off the stalk, counting each time you do so. If it takes three puffs to blow off all the seeds, it's three o'clock; four puffs, four o'clock; and so on.

This game has a serious purpose — it reminds us that some flowers' seeds, including those of the dandelion, are dispersed by the wind.

Other dandelion games include making bracelets from the stalks, and splitting the stalks to blow raspberry sounds through them.

The name 'dandelion' comes from the French 'dent de lion', meaning 'lion's tooth', because of the jagged shape of the leaves.

Make a daisy chain

There is a flower, a little flower,
With silver crest and golden eye …
JAMES MONTGOMERY

The daisy — whose name literally means 'day's eye', is surely our commonest and most familiar wild flower — but, as with so many common-or-garden things in nature, one we take for granted.

Nevertheless, this modest little flower can be used in one of the simplest of all pastimes: making a daisy chain.

The process couldn't be simpler: just pick a couple of dozen daisies, leaving the stalk as long as you can. Then use your fingernail or a sharp penknife to split each stalk halfway along, and thread the next daisy through the gap. Carry on until you have enough for a bracelet, necklace or even a skipping rope.

It's sometimes said that spring hasn't really arrived until you can cover nine daisies with your foot.

Make things from rose petals

Every June and July, the front garden of the house I grew up in was filled with the scent of roses. Like many children, I couldn't resist crushing up the petals in a jar full of water to make 'perfume' for my mother. I'm not sure she appreciated the destruction I wrought on her lovely roses in order to make this rather smelly concoction, but to me it brought a touch of the exotic to our suburban lives.

If you want to make something more practical and long-lasting out of rose petals or other garden flowers, how about a potpourri? It's simple to do and can achieve very satisfying results — an ideal birthday present, for instance.

What to do

⚙ In late summer, just as the flowers mature, pick a selection of different petals from different coloured plants (which also gives you a mixture of different scents). Timing is important — you must pick them before they turn brown.

- Dry the petals, either by leaving them on a tray or by baking them in the oven at a very low heat.
- Using a large jar (old-fashioned Kilner jars with their sealable tops are ideal), put in your ingredients in layers:
- Rose petals or those from other garden flowers.
- A 'fixative' such as dried lavender, oak moss or orrisroot (available from herbalists or by mail order).
- Spices: cinnamon, cloves and nutmeg are excellent as they give a really distinctive, woody scent.
- A few drops of essential oil such as lavender (or, if you prefer, perfume) to intensify the scent.
- Seal the jar and leave for a couple of weeks, shaking it every day or two to mix up the contents.
- Then either sew it into the lining of cushion covers or pillows, or put in an open dish to allow the scent to fill a room.

You can also make rose-petal sandwiches

- Pick a bunch of rose petals and remove the white part at the base.
- Take a 250g slab of butter, wrap it first in the rose petals, then in kitchen foil or cling-film and leave overnight in a cool place.
- The next morning, spread the 'rose butter' on to two thin slices of white bread, add a layer of rose petals to one slice, and sprinkle with a little caster sugar.
- Top with the other slice of bread and cut in half.
- Eat.

Put a buttercup under your chin to see if you like butter

This is another classic childhood custom that is in danger of dying out, which would be a pity. Just find a field of buttercups, pick one, and place it under your little brother's or sister's chin. Then it's your turn. If there's a yellow patch under your chin when you do so, you like butter — and there always is!

This game appears to have originated from the widespread belief that the rich yellow colour of butter came because cows ate buttercups — though in fact the buttercup is bitter-tasting, so cattle and other grazing animals avoid it.

The meadow buttercup, the commonest British species, has declined in recent years because of the loss of so many of our traditional hay meadows. The closely related corn buttercup has suffered even more: it has disappeared from four-fifths of its range in the past thirty years.

Beside the seaside

Who can forget summer holidays by the sea, when we paddled along the shore, explored the wonders of rock pools, felt the warm sand between our toes and enjoyed endless sunshine and freedom ...?

Today, some children have never been to a British seaside. Yet nowhere in this country is more than 112 kilometres (about 70 miles) from the coast — less than two hours' drive. So there really is no excuse for not making at least one trip to the seaside every summer ...

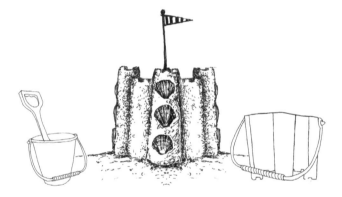

Build a sandcastle

This is your chance to become king or queen for a day — making your very own Camelot out of sand. There really are no limits to what you can achieve — from a simple bucket-shaped tower with a flag stuck on top to a whole complex of fortifications, turrets, moats and drawbridges.

What you need

- Buckets — ideally a set ranging in size from large to small.
- Spades — basic plastic ones will do, but wooden ones with a metal blade give a cleaner cut and won't break.

- Plastic knives to smooth the surface of your sandcastle.
- Stuff to decorate the finished structure — flags, shells, pebbles, bits of driftwood, plastic toys …
- And, of course, sand — fairly wet stuff works best, as you can mould it into shapes easily without it collapsing or crumbling.

The best time to make a sandcastle is just as the tide is going out, when the sand a few feet above the tideline is still quite wet.

How to build it

- Start by drawing a circle in the sand — from about one metre to three or four metres across.
- Then start to excavate the moat for your castle, digging down into the sand around the edge of your circle, to a depth of between 20 and 30cm.
- As you dig, pile up the sand to make a wall around the inside of your moat — this will be the main wall of the castle complex.
- To make the turrets, fill your bucket up with sand, making sure it's packed in tightly at the bottom, then pat down the sand at the top of the bucket to make a smooth, flat surface.
- Turn your bucket over and give it a sharp bang on top with your spade. Then carefully lift the bucket up, wiggling it if the sand won't come out.
- If you've got the consistency of the sand just right you'll have a lovely neat sandcastle — if you haven't, try again with slightly drier or wetter sand until you find the right consistency.
- Smooth any rough edges with a plastic knife.
- Then decorate your castle with the pebbles, shells, etc., etc.
- You can also use the buckets to fill your moat with sea water.

If you've found the right place between the low and high tide-lines, you can wait and watch as the tide comes in and floods your day's work. But don't worry — you can come back and build an even better one tomorrow.

Collect seashells

Lots of holiday resorts around our coasts have shops selling exotic seashells for you to buy; but it's much more fun to make your own collection. All you need is a bucket to carry them in ...

Take a walk along any sandy beach — ideally at low tide or when the tide is dropping. As you wander along the tideline, look out for shells — either washed up on the surface or half buried in the sand. Try putting a large shell (such as a whelk) to your ear to hear the sound of the sea.

Once you've got enough in your bucket, take them to a rock pool and give them a good clean. If you come across a shell with something living inside it, take a close look, and then put it back in the rock pool.

Most of the shells you find will be common 'bivalves' (creatures whose shell divides into two halves) such as cockles or mussels. You may also find snail-like shells like the whelk, or razor shells — long, straight shells which look like an old-fashioned razor. If you're very lucky, you may even come across beautiful scallop shells.

'She sells seashells on the seashore' is one of the toughest tonguetwisters in the English language. Try saying it five times in a row without stopping.

Go on a seaweed hunt

Despite their rather dull name, the various organisms which we know as 'seaweed' are some of the most extraordinary living things on the planet.

Once considered to be lowly members of the plant kingdom, the 9,000 or so different kinds of seaweeds are now classified as algae. They come in all sorts of different shapes and sizes, many of which can be found along any stretch of beach.

Just like plants, seaweeds live and grow by the process of photosynthesis – so just like plants, they need food, water and light. That's why they mainly occur in shallow water – which is where to look for them. The best beaches for seaweeds are usually rocky ones, where the seaweeds can find a secure place to fix themselves using their 'holdfast'.

The best time to look is a low or falling tide, when you can scramble across the rocks. Watch out – weed-covered rocks can be very slippery, so wear rubber-soled shoes rather than do this with bare feet or in flipflops.

One of the most familiar seaweeds, found between the high and low tidelines on any rocky beach, is known as 'bladderwrack'. The bladders along the long, brown fronds are filled with air so that when the tide comes in the fronds lift in the water and are better able to reach up towards the light. Try popping them and see what happens …

starfish

seaweed

Seaweeds are used for all sorts of things, including food (the Welsh make a delicacy called laver bread from red seaweed and oats), fertilisers and medicine, especially in Eastern cultures. Seaweed fibre has even been made into environmentally friendly clothing such as T-shirts.

Incredibly, seaweeds are thought to be responsible for more than three-quarters of the world's photosynthesis – the process by which plants fix carbon dioxide from the atmosphere, creating the oxygen by which all animals live.

Seaweed is also used to forecast the weather – if you hang it up, and watch whether it turns damp or stays dry, you can tell if it's going to rain.

Explore rock pools by the seaside

When the tide goes out, many sea creatures risk exposure to the sun and wind which would quickly dry them out if they stayed put. So they seek refuge in rock pools — little oases of cool water where they can stay safe until the tide comes back in, and they can feed again.

So the few hours when the tide is at its lowest is a great time to explore rock pools — you'll be amazed at what you can find.

blennie

limpet

What you need

- ⚙ Containers such as plastic buckets or boxes filled with seawater (clear ones are good as they allow you to see what you have caught from all angles).
- ⚙ A small fishing net or two (usually sold at seaside shops).
- ⚙ Rubber gloves if you're fussy about handling stuff.
- ⚙ A magnifying glass to take a really close look.
- ⚙ Sturdy rubber-soled shoes or boots, as rocks may be both slippery and sharp.
- ⚙ A sun hat and/or suncream.
- ⚙ Sunglasses — especially those with polarised lenses, which make it much easier to see beneath the surface of the water on a sunny day.
- ⚙ A field guide to coastal creatures.

You can also make yourself an underwater periscope, using a large plastic drinks bottle (two-litre ones are ideal). Cut the bottom off using scissors or a sharp knife, and cover the end with a piece of cling film. Then put it most of the way into the water with the top of the bottle above the surface – and simply look through it.

Tips

- Check the tide tables to make sure you've got your timing right – remember the highest and lowest tides coincide with the full and new moon each month, and also around the time of the spring and autumn equinoxes.
- Always be aware of a rising tide so you don't get cut off as the waters return. If in doubt take local advice.
- Take your time – at first sight a rock pool may look empty, but if you watch and wait you'll soon see signs of life.
- Be gentle handling what you find – these may be living creatures with soft bodies, which can be easily damaged if you're rough with them.
- Lift stones or rocks carefully – there may be creatures hiding beneath them.
- Once you've had a good look, put things back where you found them.

What to look for

- Fish: small fish often get stranded at low tide, and have to wait until the tide comes in to get back out to sea. Other kinds of fish make a permanent home in rock pools. Use your net to catch them so you can take a closer look. The commonest kinds are blennies, gobies, rocklings and bullheads.
- Crabs: these usually scuttle away as soon as you spot them, but if you're quick – and careful – you might be able to grab one. They may also be hiding in the crevices between rocks. Look out for the hermit crab, a fascinating creature that 'borrows' an empty seashell for its mobile home.
- Sea anemones: these may look like exotic plants, but in fact they're primitive animals related to the jellyfish. Watch out for their sting – it's best to look rather than touch.

- Starfish: these creatures crawl around using their five 'arms' — actually more like legs, as they have thousands of tiny feet on the underside to enable them to move about. Their mouth is on the underside of their body.
- Limpets: try budging a limpet and you realise just how strong these little shellfish are — using a suction pad on their 'foot' to stick to the rock. But as soon as the tide comes in they detach themselves and move around looking for food — before re-turning to exactly the same spot as before.
- Barnacles: these tiny white shellfish are usually found all over the surface of a rock — use your magnifying glass to get a good view.
- Seaweeds: rocks are usually covered with a range of seaweeds, of which the commonest is bladderwrack — the one with the air sacs which you can pop to make a noise.

One member of the barnacle family, the goose barnacle, is a larger creature whose body was once thought to resemble the head and neck of a goose — hence the unusual name. Bizarrely, this led to the idea that the species known as barnacle goose actually hatched from these shells, and so should not be classified as birds, but as fish. Conveniently, this meant they could be eaten on a Friday, when eating meat was forbidden.

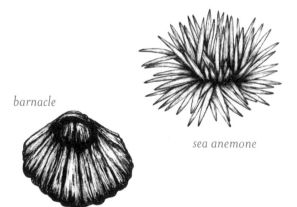

barnacle

sea anemone

hermit crab

Watch the tide go in and out during the course of a day

One of the most intriguing natural phenomena is the twice-daily rhythm of the tides, and thus the change in the appearance of a beach between high and low tide — you would never guess that you were looking at the same place on the same day.

Tides are caused by the gravitational forces of the moon (and to a lesser extent the sun), and their pull on the vast water bodies of our planet's oceans.

In Britain we are lucky to have a wide range between our high and low tides — something that gives our coastline and its beaches much of their special character.

Tidal height and depth varies from day to day and season to season. The biggest differences between low and high tide occur around the times of the new and full moon, when the gravitational pull of the sun adds its forces to those of the moon to create what are known as 'spring tides' — though despite their name they can occur at any time of year.

When the moon is in its first or third quarter, the gravitational pull is at its weakest, and the difference between high and low tide is far less: these are known as 'neap tides'.

Tides create the area between high and low tides known as the intertidal zone, which is excellent for wildlife. All kinds of marine creatures — from crabs and limpets to cockles and mussels — depend on the twice-daily changes that occur here; as do the many predators that depend on the marine life for food, especially gulls and wading birds.

But the massive changes that occur between high and low tide don't make for an easy life — just imagine if you had to live half the day under water and half the day exposed to the wind and sun. So the creatures that make their home between the tidelines must be tough, adaptable and very good at hiding.

One way to appreciate the wonder of the tides is to watch the tide go in and out in the same place on the same day. You don't necessarily have to stay put all day, but you should visit three or four times during the twelve-hour tidal cycle if you can.

- Check the local times for tides where you are, either by getting hold of a set of tide tables (usually sold at seaside shops or available free at tourist information offices, or on the Internet).
- Remember that most tide tables show times as GMT – during British Summer Time, from the end of March to the end of October, you have to add an hour. So if the tide table shows high tide at 10.23 a.m., the actual timing will be 11.23 a.m., and so on throughout the summer.
- To see a really spectacular tide, check the heights and depths of the tides on your tide table. The higher and lower the figures are (in metres) the greater the difference you will see.
- Try to be in position half an hour or so before high tide, then watch as the waters rise and reach their upper limit. You can mark this using a stick or a large rock.
- Then either wait and watch, or come back about three hours later, at mid-tide. You'll notice the difference as your high-tide mark will now be literally high and dry.
- Return again half an hour before low tide, and when you think the tide has gone out as far as it can, put another stick or rock at the lower limit. Then pace up the beach to measure the difference between the two.
- If you have time, come back again three hours later on the rising tide, and six hours later at high tide again …

Go crabbing

There are few more satisfying summer-holiday pastimes than sitting on the side of a harbour, dangling a length of fishing line into the water below, and feeling that sharp tug when you know you've caught a crab.

What you need

- A length of fishing line at least six metres long (most seaside shops sell these wound around a plastic handle).
- A small weight to tie to the end of the line, which will keep it under the water.
- Some bait – bacon rind is a favourite, but crabs aren't fussy, so any piece of meat will do. Again, many seaside shops will sell you the full kit including bait.
- A large bucket of seawater to keep the crabs in after you've caught them.

Tips

- The best places to go crabbing are sea walls, harbours or breakwaters with fairly deep water below – so make sure you don't fall in. If you can find a spot with some railings which you can tuck yourself behind, you'll probably be safer.
- High tide is usually the best time as the water will be deeper.
- Be patient. Crabs will sometimes take a few minutes to notice the bait, so don't keep pulling your fishing line in and out of the water.

- When you feel a sharp tug on the line, don't be tempted to pull it up straight away. Give the crab a chance to get hold of the bait, and then pull the line up slowly and carefully. At this point the crab might let go anyway, but with persistence you'll eventually manage to catch one.
- As you take it off the bait and put it in your bucket mind the claws — they can give you a nasty nip. The best way to hold a crab is to put your fingers and thumb either side of its shell and grip fairly tightly.
- Take a good look at the crabs you've caught, but don't handle them too much. Then put the crabs carefully back into the water.

The British Open Crabbing Championships are held every August at the seaside village of Walberswick in Suffolk. The person catching the heaviest crab within the ninety-minute time limit wins a cash prize and an engraved silver salver. Anyone can enter for a fee of just £1, but if you fall in you will be fined £10 for frightening the crabs! But it's all for a good cause: the proceeds go to local charities.

Go sea-fishing

As a boy I was a typically fussy eater, and every Friday my grandmother would have a battle to persuade me to eat the cod, haddock or plaice she had bought from the fish delivery van. All that changed when we went on holiday to Lyme Regis in Dorset, took a boat out and I caught my very own mackerel. That night, back at our boarding house, the landlady cooked it for us — and for the first time ever I cleaned my plate and asked for more. I can still remember how incredibly fresh it tasted — so good I didn't even mind the odd bone ...

Nowadays we usually buy our fish from the supermarket counter, or pre-packed in frozen fillets, steaks or fingers. But why not try catching your own for once? Sitting down to a fish supper that you've caught yourself is not only the freshest way to eat fish, but also the most satisfying.

Many holiday resorts in the south and west — Devon, Cornwall and Wales in particular — offer sea-fishing trips, with everything you need (tackle, bait, etc.) supplied. These are a great day out for all the family, with children often proving better than Mum and Dad at catching fish … Check out the tourist information office or the Internet, or just look out for boards advertising times and prices around the port or harbour.

Visit a seal colony

Seals are very impressive creatures. Slow and clumsy on land, as soon as they get into the water they are transformed into elegant undersea acrobats, reaching speeds of 20kph — easily fast enough to catch their fishy prey. In comparison, the fastest human swimmer would struggle to reach a third of that speed.

Unfortunately it's hard to observe seals in their marine habitat; we usually need to wait until they come ashore to breed to get close-up views.

The best way to see seals is to go on an organised boat trip — you'll be in the hands of experts and get great views without disturbing them at this vital time of their lives.

Where to go

The best places to watch seals are

- Norfolk (the large colony of grey and common seals on Blakeney Point).
- Northumberland (especially the Farne Islands).
- The Moray Firth on Scotland's east coast.
- The west coast of Scotland, especially around the Isle of Mull.

- West Wales, especially the Pembrokeshire coast and islands.
- Devon and Cornwall.
- Strangford Lough in Northern Ireland.

When to go

This will vary from place to place, depending on which species you want to see (common seal pups appear in spring, greys in autumn) and of course the tide times.

Boat trips usually run from April to October, and it's worth planning ahead to make the most of it.

What to look for

There are two different kinds of seal in Britain: the grey seal and the common seal. These names are a bit misleading: there are four times as many grey seals as common seals in Britain (though common are more abundant worldwide), and both kinds can appear grey in colour.

The best way to tell them apart is by their expression: common seals look rather kindly, whereas greys look as if they are squinting down their noses at you.

The grey seal is the largest resident mammal in Britain. At roughly 230kg, a male weighs in at about twice as heavy as a fully grown red deer stag.

Visit a seabird colony

Of all the natural sights in Britain, nothing beats the sheer spectacle of a seabird colony. The sight, sound and smell of thousands of seabirds packed in together on a lump of rock or cliff face really does have to be experienced to be believed.

Britain's seabird colonies are also something we can be very proud of. We may not have the hottest deserts or the deepest oceans; we can't boast of lions, tigers or polar bears; but we do play host to some of the largest and most spectacular collections of seabirds anywhere in the world.

Seabirds usually nest on remote headlands or offshore islands, to avoid their eggs and chicks being eaten by predators such as rats and foxes. So most colonies are remote and hard to reach. But if you make the effort, I can promise you won't be disappointed.

Manx shearwater   *puffin*   *gannet*

Where to go

Seabirds like rocky cliffs and islands, so most colonies are in the north and west, especially Scotland. Some of the most easily accessible colonies are

- Bempton Cliffs, near Bridlington in Yorkshire.
- The Farne Islands, reachable by boat from Seahouses in Northumberland.
- Bass Rock, viewable from boat trips from North Berwick, south of Edinburgh.
- South Stack, on the north-west corner of the Isle of Anglesey, North Wales.
- Skomer, reachable by boat from the Pembrokeshire coast in south-west Wales.
- Isles of Scilly, off Land's End in Cornwall.
- Blakeney Point, a long shingle spit in Norfolk, reachable by boat or a very long, tough walk.
- Rathlin Island, off County Antrim in Northern Ireland.

When to go

Seabirds spend the winter out in the open ocean, usually returning in March or April and beginning to breed in May, before departing with their chicks in July or August. So the best time to visit a colony is early summer between mid-May and mid-July, when nesting activity reaches its peak.

What to look for

Depending on where you go, you can expect to see the following seabirds

- Gannet: Britain's largest seabird and one of the most spectacular, as it plummets into the ocean to hunt for food at speeds of more than 100kph.
- Puffin: everyone's favourite character – the penguin-like bird with the massive colourful bill for holding the maximum number of fish.
- Guillemots and razorbills: two other members of the auk family; penguin-like seabirds which look clumsy on land but graceful under water.
- Cormorant and shag: these closely related birds lack the ability to waterproof their plumage, so often pose with their wings held out to dry.
- 'Seagulls': you may see half a dozen different kinds of gull, including the large and predatory herring and great black-backed gulls which harass other birds for their food, and also steal eggs and chicks. The ocean-going kittiwake, a more delicate-looking gull, can be heard calling out its name at many colonies.
- Terns: several different kinds of these elegant birds, also known as 'sea swallows', breed around our coasts, including common, Arctic, roseate, Sandwich and little terns. As someone once said, terns look like 'a gull that has died and gone to heaven'.

The greatest global voyager on the planet, the Arctic tern, migrates from its breeding colonies in Britain to Antarctica and back every year. Over the course of a lifetime, a single Arctic tern may travel more than 800,000 kilometres (half a million miles) — and experience more hours of daylight than any other living creature.

bottle-nosed dolphin

minke whale

Go whale- and dolphin-watching

Many people are surprised to discover that whales, dolphins and porpoises can be found off the coasts of Britain and Ireland. We usually associate these huge sea mammals with more exotic locations, but in fact many find a home in our coastal waters, especially in summer.

Although there are a few places where you can see them from the shore, to get really good views you usually need to take a boat trip out into the open sea. Nowadays there are quite a few specialist companies that run whale-watching trips, mostly off our western and northern coasts.

Tips

⚙ Remember, even in summer, it is always cooler at sea than on land, so wrap up warm.
⚙ Take plenty of suncream even if it's cloudy — you burn more easily at sea.
⚙ Take binoculars and a camera.

- To avoid seasickness it's usually best to eat little and often, stay on deck and stare at the horizon.
- Look out for flocks of seabirds gathering over the water. Seabirds mean fish, and where there are fish, there may also be whales or dolphins hunting for them.

Where to go

The main hotspots are in the south-west, Wales and Scotland, including

- Devon and Cornwall.
- Pembrokeshire.
- The Western Isles of Scotland (e.g. Mull, Skye).
- Shetland and Orkney.
- Strangford Lough in Northern Ireland.
- Cape Clear Island and the headlands of County Cork.
- The Moray Firth in eastern Scotland – where you can even watch the antics of bottle-nosed dolphins from the shore.

And if you're really keen

Take a car and passenger ferry across the Bay of Biscay to northern Spain. The Bay of Biscay, off the west coast of France, is one of the very best places to see whales and other marine mammals in the world, and several whale-watching companies run trips.

When to go

Whales, dolphins and porpoises can be seen in British waters all year round, but the highest numbers occur from spring to autumn. Peak months are generally July to September, so whale-watching is a great thing to do on your summer holidays.

Calm, windless days are best – not just because you're less

likely to get seasick, but also because it's much easier to spot sea mammals when the surface of the sea is not too choppy. Cloudy days are better than sunny, as glare reduces your chance of spotting a fin – but as you don't usually have much choice about the British weather you may have to take pot luck.

harbour porpoise

sunfish

basking shark

What to look for

⚙ Bottle-nosed dolphin: the commonest dolphin in British waters, with a distinctive friendly expression, and often seen in large groups known as 'pods'. Hotspots include the Moray Firth and west Wales.

⚙ Harbour porpoise: smaller, more solitary and less playful than the bottle-nosed dolphin, with a blunter snout. Found off all our coasts, but commoner in the north and west.

⚙ Minke whale: a small- to medium-sized whale, and the commonest in British waters, especially off north-west Scotland. If you're really lucky you may see minke whales leaping out of the water.

You may also see other sea creatures, including:

⚙ Seabirds: especially gannets, puffins and (off west Wales and the Hebrides) Manx shearwaters.

- Basking sharks: especially in late summer off Cornwall, the west coast of Scotland and south-west Ireland. The basking shark is the world's second largest fish, but despite its huge size is harmless to humans.
- Sunfish: these huge, round fish bask on the surface of the water.

The largest creature that has ever lived on Earth, the Blue Whale, is very occasionally seen in British waters — though as with all ocean-going animals the sightings are very hard to predict.

Summer weather lore

St Swithun's Day — July 15 — is surely the best-known date in the weather calendar. As the old rhyme says:

St Swithun's Day if it do rain,
For forty days it will remain;
St Swithun's Day if it be fair,
For forty days will rain no more.

It's a nice idea — but does it work? Well, generally, no. Even in the wettest summer on record, 2007, there was the occasional fine day in the forty-day period after St Swithun's Day. But in the long hot summer of 1976 there were parts of southern England where it did not rain at all from the Whitsun bank holiday at the end of May to the August one: about ninety days.

The reason our ancestors needed proverbs like that of St Swithun to predict the summer weather was because they didn't have any proper weather forecasters, so had to rely on a mixture of folklore and old wives' tales. This was a particularly crucial time of year because of the annual harvest, which if it failed could lead to starvation the following winter.

So most people looked forward to the period known as the

'dog days', which begins in early July and ends in mid-August. This relates to the appearance at dawn of the brightest star in the heavens, Sirius, which is supposed to coincide with a spell of calm, settled weather.

People also used observations of natural events, and the behaviour of birds in particular, to help them forecast the weather. The habits of swallows were especially important, and gave rise to a well-known proverb:

Swallows high, staying dry;
Swallows low, wet will blow.

This has a real basis in fact. Watch swallows, house martins or swifts on a fine summer's evening, as they hawk for insects in a darkening sky. The reason the birds are flying so high is that the insects on which they are feeding are carried up into the warm, settled air by thermal currents.

On the other hand, if the birds are flying low, it is because the air currents are being disturbed, keeping the insects low too; and this usually signals a change to cooler, less settled weather.

So next time you see these graceful birds hunting for insects at dusk, check out where they're flying, and see what the weather is like the next day …

Autumn

Season of mists and mellow fruitfulness,
Close bosom-friend of the maturing sun,
Conspiring with him how to load and bless
With fruit the vines that round the thatch-eves run …

JOHN KEATS

The nights may be drawing in, and it's getting colder, but autumn is still one of the best seasons to be out and about and getting back to nature. Conker fights in the playground, picking blackberries or searching for mushrooms are just some of the many things you can do at this time of year.

Autumn is a busy time for wildlife, too. With winter fast approaching, plants and animals have to take rapid action if they are going to survive the coming cold weather.

Swallows and house martins migrate, heading away from our shores to spend the winter in Africa. Their place is taken by winter thrushes from the north, feasting on the glut of berries in our hedgerows, and swans and geese on our coastal marshes. Flowers and trees are packed with fruit, nuts and seeds, spiders are building their webs, and tawny owls are hooting to defend their winter territory.

But it's not all about getting ready for the winter. Our largest land mammal, the red deer, is in the middle of its courtship season, with rival males challenging each other for the right to mate with the most females, in the famous annual deer rut.

Autumn is also a great time to make things: build a nest box, dig a pond or collect some seeds and plant a tree – the fruits of your labours will pay off in the year ahead. So go on, wrap up warm, get out there and enjoy yourself!

Have a conker fight

The end of the long summer holidays brings the return to school, to a chorus of moans and groans from children all over the country. But in the past there was one silver lining: the chance to play conkers. We could hardly wait until the horse chestnuts fell from the tree and burst out of their prickly green casings, revealing the magnificent shiny brown conkers within. Bruised knuckles and the occasional bash in the face were well worth it for the joy of seeing your conker defeat all comers at playtime. What a pity that some misguided busybodies have decided to ban conker fights from school playgrounds.

How to play

All you need is a thin piece of string about 30cm long, a thin meat skewer to make the hole — and of course a nice, big conker.

* Look for the roundest, most symmetrical conker you can find, making sure it doesn't have any cracks or splits.
* Using the skewer, make a neat hole in the top of the conker, pushing carefully right the way through to the other side. Try to keep the hole as narrow as possible.
* Feed through your string, and tie a large knot at the bottom to hold it in place.
* Trim off any excess string at the bottom, and you're ready to play …

The rules

1. Your opponent hangs their conker down from the string wrapped around their hand, holding it as steadily as they can.
2. You wrap your own piece of string around your hand, then swing your conker down to hit your opponent's one as hard as you can. If you miss you are allowed two more goes.

3. If the strings get tangled up, the first player to call 'Strings' gets a bonus shot.
4. If either of you drops your conker, the other player can shout 'Stamps!' and jump on it; but not if its owner has already cried 'No stamps!'
5. The game goes on until one of the conkers either falls off its string or is broken.

The winning conker then becomes a 'one-er' — meaning that it has beaten one other conker. Each time it wins a contest, it adds another one to its score, becoming a 'two-er', 'three-er' and so on.

But ... if your conker beats another one that is already, say, a 'five-er', you add that score to your own, plus one more for winning. So your 'one-er' becomes a 'seven-er'. A really great conker might eventually become a 'fifty-er' or even a 'hundred-er'!

How to strengthen your conker

Opinions differ on what you should do to make your conker as strong as possible. Here are just a few suggestions (and reasons why they might not work!).

* Bake your conkers in the oven at 140° C (gas mark 1) for about two hours (though some people say that makes them brittle).
* Pickle your conkers in vinegar (though some say this rots the inside).
* Smear your conkers with Oil of Olay (a face cream) – this doesn't make them hard, but softens them, the theory being that they absorb the impact of your rival's conker ...

And my favourite:

* Feed your conker to a pig, and wait until it comes out the other end. It will be unbeatable.

But there is a much simpler method:

✳ Put your conkers in a drawer and forget about them until next autumn (making sure you put the string on first otherwise you'll have to use a drill when you get them out again). The resulting conker will be small, dark and shrivelled — and tough as old boots!

When you find the first conker of the autumn, it will bring you luck if you say: 'Obli obli onker, my first conker!' (Or alternatively, 'Ibbley ibbley ack, my first crack!')

The World Conker Championship is held every year, on the second Sunday of October, on the village green at Ashton, in Northamptonshire.

The word 'conker' may derive from 'conqueror' — referring to a winning nut; or it may come from the French word 'cogner', meaning to hit or bash. The first recorded game of conkers took place in 1848, although a similar game was played much earlier — using hazelnuts or live snails.

Collect and roast sweet chestnuts

You can't eat conkers — and you will be pretty sick if you try — but nuts from their close relative the sweet chestnut are very tasty and can be used in all sorts of recipes. Like the horse chestnut, the sweet chestnut is not a native tree — it was probably brought to Britain by the Romans who ground the nuts down to make flour. It's quite easy to tell the difference — sweet-chestnut cases are very prickly to touch, with much finer and longer spikes than those of the horse chestnut, and the sweet chestnut inside has a pointed top, while the horse chestnut is much rounder and smooth.

Roasted is the nicest way to eat sweet chestnuts, and also the simplest. Once you've collected them (any time from late October through to December), puncture the shell of each one with a sharp skewer or fork, or cut a cross-shaped slit across the top (to stop them exploding. This also makes them easier to peel.)

If you have one, an open fire is best for roasting, as the smoke gives the nuts a real flavour. If not, an oven will work just as well. Just put them in a roasting tin and cook for half an hour or so at 200° C or gas mark 6.

Once roasted and peeled, you can use them in cakes, stews and soups; or as the basis of a stuffing for the Christmas turkey – or just eat them as they are.

Pick (and eat) blackberries

During the Second World War fresh fruit was hard to get, so blackberries were a welcome addition to the meagre wartime diet. My grandmother told me that one day a neighbour called round with some blackberries, and started to hand them round for the children to eat, without washing them first. My grandmother was horrified. 'Won't they have maggots in them?' she asked. 'Maybe,' replied her neighbour as the children stuffed their faces with the juicy fruit. 'But the way I sees it, them that eats most blackberries, gets most maggots!'

Blackberries are the best free food in the countryside – easy to find, easy to pick (as long as you're careful of the prickles on the bramble bushes) and great to eat.

The first ripe blackberries appear about the time of the Wimbledon tennis tournament in early July, but there aren't usually enough to make them worth picking until August or September. Unripe blackberries are small, hard and either green or red – so wait until you can see big bunches of black ones before you go on a picking expedition.

Take a container to put them in, and a pair of thin but strong gardening gloves to avoid your hands being pricked or stained – though some people don't mind getting a bit messy.

And try not to eat too many while you're picking them – it'll take you twice as long to collect enough to make something delicious once you get them home.

It's said in some parts of Britain that the first blackberry of the season to be spotted and eaten will banish warts, and in other parts that some time around early October the devil spits (or in some versions of the story, pees) on blackberries so they are no longer good to eat. This last myth probably arose because later in the season you often get tiny worms in the fruit, making them unpleasant tasting.

Some easy blackberry recipes

BLACKBERRY AND APPLE CRUMBLE
* Mix 200g plain flour and 100g cold butter (chopped up into cubes) into a bowl until they are crumbled; then mix in 100g sugar.
* Wash 1kg apples, remove the cores and peel and slice them, then arrange in the bottom of a large shallow dish.

* Wash a couple of handfuls of blackberries, pat them dry, and then put them on top of the apple slices.
* Sprinkle 100g of demerara sugar over the fruit.
* Spread the crumble mixture evenly on top.
* Cook at 180° C (gas mark 4) for 40–50 minutes, until the topping goes nice and brown.
* Tastes great with cream, ice cream, custard or crème fraîche.

BLACKBERRY FOOL

* Purée 300g of blackberries with 75–100g of sugar in a blender, then push through a sieve to remove the pips.
* Add the juice of a lemon (to taste).
* Whisk 180ml of double cream until it starts to thicken.
* Fold the cream into the blackberry purée.
* Garnish with a few fresh blackberries and serve.

BLACKBERRY JELLY

This is a really good one as it's one of the few jams that doesn't need extra pectin in order to set – the blackberries themselves contain enough.

* Wash 500g of cooking apples (Bramleys are best) and cut them into quarters. You don't need to peel or core them.
* Put the apples into a saucepan with one litre of water and the juice of a lemon, and stew them gently over a low heat until they go soft.
* While the apples are cooking, wash 2kg blackberries and pat them dry.

* Add the blackberries to the apples and cook them until the mixture goes soft.
* Turn the mixture into a muslin bag suspended over a second clean pan, and leave overnight.
* Next day, add 300g of sugar for every half-litre of juice, giving the mixture a good stir until the sugar has dissolved completely.
* Sterilise some jars by washing them thoroughly and drying them in the oven at 100° C (gas mark ¼) for about half an hour.
* Bring the juice and sugar mixture to the boil and simmer gently, stirring from time to time, for about 10–15 minutes.
* Test whether the jelly is set by dipping a very cold teaspoon into the mixture. If, a few seconds after you take the spoon out of the pan, it starts to look like jam, the jelly is ready.
* Pour the mixture into the warm jars, cover them and leave to cool.

Watch birds feeding on fruit and berries

Birds love berries — especially in autumn when they need to build up their energy levels to be ready for the coming cold weather. But berries love birds too — or at least the trees and bushes that produce them do.

That's because after a bird has eaten a berry, and taken all the goodness from the fleshy pulp around the seeds, those seeds come out the other end of the bird. And because birds travel, the seeds may be dropped a long way from wherever they were eaten — enabling the parent plant to spread into new areas.

That's why berries look so delicious. The bright colours (especially red) have evolved to entice birds to feed on them; and the soft flesh of an elderberry or blackberry is the bird's reward for helping to spread those precious seeds. A word of warning, though — some delicious-looking berries can be eaten by birds but are poisonous to us.

Over generations, birds and berry-bearing plants have grown

to depend on each other. Thrushes, blackbirds and robins in particular need a good berry crop in order to survive the winter — and this provides us with the ideal opportunity to watch the birds at close quarters.

Tips

* As soon as the weather turns cold, stake out a berry bush and watch what comes to feed. Likely species are mistle thrush (larger, paler and more strongly marked than the song thrush), blackbird, starling and robin. Watch how these birds — especially mistle thrushes — will defend their bush against any intruders.
* In September look out for summer visitors such as white-throats and blackcaps, which feed on berries to give them energy for their long journey south.
* From October onwards keep an eye out for two winter thrushes: the fieldfare and redwing. Both come from Scandinavia and northern Russia to take advantage of the plentiful food and mild winter climate we offer. Fieldfares are large, with a grey head, rufous back and wings and yellowish chest. Redwings are smaller, with a creamy eye stripe and orange-red patch on the sides.
* If you live in the east of the country, especially along the coast, you may see flocks of waxwings. These beautiful visitors from the north love red berries and are sometimes seen on exotic shrubs in supermarket car parks.

* Towards Christmas, when most berries have been eaten, look for holly and ivy berries which appear later than others, and provide a much-needed food supply for hungry birds at this time of year.
* Fallen fruit such as apples also attracts thrushes and blackbirds — so don't clear it away.

How many berries do birds eat? Assuming a wintering population of 20 million berry-eating birds, eating about five hundred berries a day each for roughly one hundred days between Christmas and Easter — and the astonishing answer is 1,000,000,000,000 berries — or, if you prefer, one trillion. And that's just in a single winter …

Go on a 'fungal foray'

Fungi are bizarre things. Neither plant nor animal, they are among the largest living creatures on the planet, stretching for miles underground. But the only part of this vast organism we see is its fruit: the mushrooms and toadstools that appear — as if by magic — in our woods and fields every autumn.

Many people are put off searching for fungi because they're worried about being poisoned. But as long as you're careful and sensible — and don't pick or eat any fungus you aren't absolutely sure of — you will be perfectly safe. If you aren't confident about whether a mushroom is poisonous or not, then don't touch it.

To discover more about our fascinating fungi, why not go on a 'fungal foray' — either on your own or on an organised walk with an expert to guide you? Many Wildlife Trusts, local councils and fungi groups run these events during the autumn months. You'll be amazed at the hidden secrets behind these weird and wonderful organisms …

orange peel

stinkhorn

razor-strop fungus

king alfred's cake

shaggy ink-cup

witches butter

hoof fungus

When to go

Fungi generally appear in the autumn, and the best time to look for them is early in the morning on a mild, cloudy day from September through to early November, depending on where in the country you live.

Where to go

Fungi can be found almost anywhere – though they prefer damp places where they can obtain precious nutrients from the soil or from other decaying material such as rotten trees.

Woods are always a good place to look – don't forget that many kinds of fungi, such as the bracket fungus, actually grow on the tree itself. The edges of fields and beneath hedgerows are also fungal hotspots. You may even get some growing on your back lawn.

What to take

* Gloves if you want to handle fungi.
* A field guide to help you identify what you find.
* A digital camera.

What's the difference between a mushroom and a toadstool? There isn't one. However, we generally use the term 'toadstool' to refer to poisonous fungi, and 'mushroom' for those we can eat.

Fungi have some really odd names – look at these for starters:

* Orange Peel: named because it looks just like the discarded skin of an orange.
* King Alfred's Cake: found on dead wood, appears burnt on the surface.
* Hoof Fungus: looks exactly like a horse's hoof.
* Shaggy Ink-cap: egg-shaped fungus with shaggy blue frills.
* Stinkhorn: leaves little to the imagination …
* Witches' Butter: appears as black blobs on the branches of oak trees.
* Razor-strop Fungus: apparently so named because when dried it could be used to sharpen an old-fashioned cut-throat razor.

There are all sorts of bizarre beliefs and old wives' tales about how to tell a poison-ous fungus from an edible one. These include the idea that any mushroom that peels is edible (wrong); that all mushrooms collected from fields are edible (wrong); or that if you boil a mushroom with a silver spoon, and the spoon turns black, the mushroom is poisonous (also wrong).

Collect seeds and plant a tree

Collecting seeds — then planting them — is one of the best ways to learn about how nature works. It's also easy to do and good fun. You can start by collecting seeds from plants in your garden or local wood; then go on to look for tree seeds such as acorns, beech nuts or pine cones, and plant a tree.

Collecting flower seeds

From late summer into autumn, many wild flowers begin to set seed, ensuring that the following spring and summer the coun-tryside will once again be awash with colour as they come into bloom. You can be part of this natural cycle by collecting flower seeds for yourself, planting them, and watching them grow.

When to go

Most plants set seed in late summer and early autumn, so this is the ideal time for seed collecting. Good ones to collect include poppies, cornflowers and nasturtiums.

What to do

* Look for plants whose flowers have already fallen off and where the seed heads are showing.
* Check for ripeness: if the seed heads are still green they aren't ready yet; if they've turned brown and rattle when you shake them, they are.
* Pick the seed heads and put them into an envelope — using a different envelope for each kind of plant. Write the name of the plant on the outside of the envelope.
* Leave them somewhere warm and dry (an airing cupboard is ideal).
* When the seed heads are completely dry, shake them over a piece of paper so the seeds fall out. You may need to sieve them to get rid of the chaff.
* Then place these back in the envelope until the spring, when it's time to plant them.

Collecting tree seeds

Visiting a wood in autumn to collect tree seeds is a great day out for all the family. All you need is something to put the seeds in and a guide to recognising which seeds come from which tree.

Good seeds to look for and collect are

* Beech nuts.
* Hazel nuts.
* Acorns (from oak trees).
* Sweet chestnuts.
* Seeds from alder cones.
* Seeds from Scots pine cones.

When you get home, you should check if your acorns, beech or hazel nuts are fertile. A good way is to put them in a bucket of water and see if they sink or float. Throw away any that float as they will not germinate.

Then you can plant your seeds straight away.

What you need

* Some containers for growing (buy at your local garden centre, or just use old flowerpots or yogurt pots).
* Compost and sand to grow them in.
* Labels to mark the containers so you know which seed is which.

What to do

* Fill your container with a mixture of compost and sand, and then plant your seeds — the nuts and acorns should be sown a couple of centimetres below the surface, while the alder and pine seeds can be sown almost at the top.
* Once you've planted each seed make sure you write a label so you don't forget what you've sown. Then leave the containers in a cool, shady spot (a shed or garage is ideal) until the spring.
* By springtime the seeds should have begun to germinate, and you will have a tiny plant in each container. Water them carefully — not too much or they'll get too wet, but enough to stop them drying out.
* When they are about 20–30cm tall it's time to plant them — find a suitable spot in the corner of your garden and don't put them too close together. Clearing weeds away and putting some mulch or compost around the base will help them grow.

Make leaf rubbings

Making leaf rubbings is a classic autumn activity that, like so many other traditional outdoor pastimes, has declined in recent years. Yet it's one of the easiest ways to make your own wrapping paper or gift cards.

First, collect your leaves

Visit a local park or woodland and collect a range of different fallen leaves. If you can, make a note of which leaf comes from which kind of tree.

Then, make leaf rubbings

* Once your leaf has completely dried out, place it upside down on a piece of card (with the veins facing upwards).
* Place a piece of white or coloured paper on top, and holding it down firmly, rub the paper with pencil, crayon or a piece of charcoal.
* You will start to see the pattern of the leaf appear on the paper. Make sure you rub over the whole of the leaf, and then lift the paper off.

* You can make different-coloured patterns or use different leaves to make a pattern, then paste into a scrapbook or hang up on the wall or fridge door. Or cut round the edge of the leaf rubbing and use in a collage (see below).

Other things you can do with leaves

LEAF PRINTS
Using a paint roller, spread paint smoothly over the surface of the leaf making sure it is completely covered. Then turn the leaf over and press it firmly on to the surface of some plain white or coloured paper. Hang it up to dry and hey presto! You have a leaf print.

LEAF COLLAGES
Using paste, stick the leaves (or your leaf rubbings) on to white or coloured paper to form patterns. Try overlapping them to form 3-D layers, or using different-coloured leaves to form shapes and patterns. Once your collage is finished put it under a pile of books so that the leaves dry and stay stuck to the paper.

LEAF T-SHIRTS
You can do your leaf collage straight on to a plain white T-shirt — using special fabric paint meaning you can wash the T-shirt when it gets dirty — then hang it up to dry.

Listen for tawny owls hooting

As the cold autumn nights draw in, I love hearing the hooting of the tawny owl in the trees around our Somerset home; a reminder of listening to owls at night when I was a child. A spooky sound, but a strangely comforting one.

The tawny is our commonest and most widespread owl, found in woodland habitats across most of lowland England, Wales and Scotland – although not in Ireland. Yet because it is almost entirely nocturnal – only emerging to hunt at night – we hardly ever see it.

But at this time of year, we can *hear* it. Tawny owls hoot a lot in autumn because the youngsters hatched back in the spring are trying to muscle in on their parents' territory. Meanwhile, Mum and Dad are trying to push Junior out into the big wide world.

One thing we all know – or at least think we know – about tawny owls is that they call 'to-whit, to-whooo'. Except they don't.

In fact, the male and female owls have quite different calls: the female has a loud 'kee-wick', while the male does the classic hoot: 'hooooo … hoo-hoo-hoo hoooooo'.

So what we are actually hearing is a duet between the pair, occasionally interrupted by the sulky teenager …

To listen for owls, choose a calm, windless night between September and November, ideally when it's cold and clear – owls don't like rain either. Wait until darkness falls, then visit a local wood. You can wander about, but you're more likely to hear the birds – and be able to work out where the sound is coming from – if you stand still.

Once you hear the hooting (or the female's shrill call), move towards the source of the sound. But take care – you don't want to frighten the birds. Then just close your eyes and listen to one of the great sounds of the British countryside.

Tip

Cup your hands behind your ears and stand facing the direction where the call is coming from. This will amplify the sound and help you pinpoint where the owl is sitting. This works well with any birdsong so you can try it out in spring as well.

Tawny owls have one of the smallest home territories of any bird – rarely venturing more than a kilometre or so away from their home for the whole of their lives.

Look for spiders in your house

Autumn is a very good time to look for spiders — or a very bad time if you're scared of them!

One of our largest spiders, the fearsome, black *Tegenaria* or house spider, becomes a lot more noticeable in late summer and autumn when the males start to go walkabout to look for females to mate with.

At this time of year they can turn up anywhere — walking across the sitting-room carpet, sitting on your duvet, or of course in the bath. By the way, it's a myth that spiders crawl up the plughole — once they've fallen in, they can't climb up the slippery sides without a helping hand from us.

Another spider found in many of our homes, but often overlooked, is the daddy-long-legs spider. It's called that because it looks just like the insect known as the 'daddy-long-legs' (also called the crane fly). This harmless and unobtrusive creature sits quite still in an untidy, tangled web in the corner of the room, where the ceiling meets the wall. Until you take a closer look, you will probably think the web is empty, as the spider that lives there is so thin and weedy it's very hard to spot.

But take a pencil, give the web a gentle prod, and the spider suddenly starts to vibrate rapidly up and down — its way of fooling other spiders which might make a meal of it. If attacked, the spider will also use its long legs to throw strands of web at the intruder to fend it off.

By sitting so quietly in what looks like a few tangled bits of web, the daddy-long-legs spider catches many an unwary insect; and will even eat other spiders, including its own kind. The offspring keep out of each other's way too, for fear that they might be munched by a sibling.

The daddy-long-legs spider is not native to Britain — it originated in mainland Europe. But it has spread throughout southern England and as far north as Yorkshire by one simple method: it makes its web in pieces of furniture like wardrobes, which are then loaded into removal vans and driven around the country.

It is sometimes said that the daddy-long-legs spider is the most poisonous creature on the planet, and that if its jaws were able to pierce human skin it could kill us in seconds. Fortunately this is completely untrue.

Look for spiders' webs on an autumn morning

A fine autumn morning is the ideal time to go looking for spiderwebs. If it's cold and clear, dew will form along the individual strands making them easier to see. Try standing behind the web as it is backlit by the rays of the early-morning sun — truly magical!

Amazing facts about spiders and their webs ...

⁎ There are about 35,000 different kinds of spider in the world — of which about six hundred are found in Britain.

⁎ The silk spiders use to make their webs is — weight for weight — stronger than steel.

⁎ A typical web is made of silk about 1/200 of a millimetre across.

⁎ If you look really closely at a spiderweb you'll see little sticky blobs — these are what the spider uses to catch its prey.

⁎ One of our smallest birds, the long-tailed tit, uses spiderwebs to make its barrel-shaped nest.

⁎ Some male spiders twang their webs like a guitar to attract a mate.

⁎ When a fly or other insect lands in a web, the spider can tell where the insect is by feeling its movements through the strands of the web.

Another thing to look out for at this time of year is the natural phenomenon known as gossamer. These are the fine silken threads that appear, as if by magic, draped across bushes and grass on fresh, clear autumn mornings.

Gossamer is actually spun by tiny baby spiders (also known as 'spiderlings'). They then launch themselves into the air and float away on individual lines of web to find a new place to live.

These delicate but incredibly strong strands enable the spiderlings to travel vast distances — several hundred kilometres away, and up to 3,000 metres above the ground in the space of one day.

The word 'gossamer' is thought to come from the phrase 'goose summer', and derives from the idea that these fine strands of silk were actually goose down.

Make a woodpile in your garden

This will create a hidden haven for wild creatures such as woodlice, bumblebees, frogs and newts, hedgehogs, wood mice and maybe even slow-worms. All sorts of fungi might appear, while if you're really fortunate you may be providing a home for the larvae of one of our biggest and most impressive insects — the stag beetle.

What to do

* Go to a local wood and look out for logs and dead branches.
* Bring them home and pile them up in a quiet corner of your garden — ideally somewhere shady and a bit damp, such as under trees or shrubs.
* Wait for the wildlife to arrive …

A stag beetle spends up to seven years underground in the form of a larva, before pupating in autumn, and emerging the following summer as a flying adult. Adult stag beetles enjoy their freedom for just a few weeks: fighting, mating, laying eggs and then dying before the summer is over. In medieval times, peasants believed that stag beetles had the power to summon thunder and lightning, and carried hot coals in their jaws, dropping them to set fire to buildings.

Give a hedgehog a helping hand

Hedgehogs are surely one of the most delightful British animals. They are also in big trouble — numbers have dropped because many of their traditional habitats have disappeared, there's less food for them to eat, and there's the constant risk of being run over and squashed on our roads.

In fact, if the current decline continues there is a real danger that the hedgehog will disappear in the next few years. So they need all the help they can get.

Autumn is the critical time of year for hedgehogs as they are getting themselves ready for their long winter hibernation — apart from bats, and the aptly named dormouse, the hedgehog is the only British mammal which sleeps right through the winter.

But before they can do so, they need to find a place to build their den — and that's when the danger is greatest. Many head to the nearest pile of logs — not realising that this is a bonfire which will be lit on 5 November to celebrate Guy Fawkes Night. So in the week leading up to the fireworks parties it's well worth checking out any bonfires to make sure there are no hedgehogs hidden inside.

If you do find one, put it in a high-sided box so it can't escape, along with a hot-water bottle wrapped in a towel or old cloth to keep it nice and warm. Give it some water to drink and meal-worms or cat food to eat; then take it back home to your garden.

Before you let it go, rake up grass cuttings, twigs or autumn leaves into a pile in a quiet corner of your garden, then tuck the hedgehog inside so it can make a new den for the winter.

How to identify ...
small mammals

Small mammals are among the commonest creatures in Britain — yet are also often very difficult to see. Even when you do catch a glimpse of them, it's usually just the sight of a rapidly disappearing, furry rear end. There are two main groups of small mammals (apart from bats) in Britain: rodents (rats, mice and voles) and insectivores (shrews, moles and hedgehogs). Some are much easier to see than others, and if you want to get good views, you'll have to be very patient.

How to identify ...
small mammals

Hedgehog

One of our favourite animals, and deservedly popular: its endearing habits and liking for slugs make it every gardener's friend. Getting much scarcer nowadays, and often in danger from traffic. Hibernates all winter, usually emerging from April to October.

Mole

One of our best-known yet least seen mammals, because of its habit of spending most of its life underground. Evidence of moles (molehills) is easy to see, especially on a neat lawn. Most likely to be seen in spring when males look for females.

Common Shrew

Like all shrews, small and incredibly active, always searching for insects to eat and only resting for a few minutes at a time. Has poor eyesight, so uses long snout to sniff out its prey. Dark brown in colour, pale underneath, with large feet and long nose.

Pygmy Shrew

Our tiniest mammal – only about 7–10 centimetres long and weighing just a few grams. Very common, and constantly active like other shrews – but hard to see. Small size and greyish-brown fur are best identification points.

Water Shrew

Our only venomous mammal, with poisonous saliva to kill its aquatic prey. Lives in and alongside shallow water, and can be seen hunting – like other shrews is continually active. Darker than other small mammals, with blackish upperparts and paler below.

Dormouse

One of our cutest but most elusive mammals, as it sleeps for more than half the year, and spends the rest of its life high in the canopy of woodlands searching for plant and insect food. Plump and with a long, bushy tail, which it uses with its powerful legs to clamber about the treetops.

Water Vole

Ratty of *Wind in the Willows* fame — but now better known for being our most rapidly declining mammal, because of losing its watery habitats and being hunted by the introduced North American mink. Plump and furry, with smaller ears and a shorter snout and tail than the brown rat. Always found near water — either on the bank or swimming — on rivers, canals and freshwater marshes.

Brown Rat

Not our most popular animal, but a fascinating one — if only because it is so successful. Easily identified by its large size, pointed snout and long, naked tail. Can be found almost anywhere with food to eat; often seen under bird tables picking up spilt seeds and nuts.

House Mouse

The classic mouse of 'Three Blind Mice' fame: small, grey and very fast. Generally confined to the inside of homes, but also found in farmyards, especially where there is grain to feed on.

Field Vole

Our commonest mammal, yet very hard to see, as it hides away from its many predators. Small, plump and furry — like a miniature water vole — but found mainly in woods and on farmland, or, increasingly nowadays, along grassy roadside verges.

Harvest Mouse

Our smallest rodent, and second only to the pygmy shrew in size: about 10–15 centimetres long and weighing from 6–11 grams — less than half an ounce. Found, as its name suggests, in farm crops; but also surprisingly common in wetlands, where it weaves its nest among reeds. Golden fur, pale belly and short ears; but most obvious feature is the tail with which it clings to grass and wheat stems like a monkey.

Wood Mouse

The mouse most likely to be seen feeding under or on your garden bird table: small, with a large head and eyes, short body and long, rounded ears — giving it a more attractive appearance than the house mouse.

Other ways to encourage hedgehogs into your garden

* Don't use pesticides, especially slug pellets, which contain enough poison to kill a healthy hedgehog. In fact any garden chemical can be harmful as they concentrate in the creatures the hedgehogs eat.
* Make a compost heap (see page 150) – these are ideal places for hedgehogs to forage for food.
* Put food out – but *not* bread and milk, which gives them indigestion. Mealworms and dog or cat food (especially white meat such as chicken) are much better.
* Hedgehogs also like a drink – so put out a bowl of fresh, clean water with the food.
* Don't keep a cat – as well as killing birds, cats are lethal to baby hedgehogs (whose spines haven't developed enough to put off an attacker).
* If you have a garden pond, make sure that if a hedgehog falls in it can get out – bricks and ramps are helpful.
* If you are cutting the lawn, check long grass for hedgehogs first.
* Leave a hole at the bottom of your garden fence so that hedge-hogs can get out and about easily.
* If you have hedgehogs in your garden, persuade your neigh-bours to become 'hedgehog-friendly' too – these animals will wander far and wide on a typical night, visiting up to a dozen different gardens for food.

One last point: if you find a hedgehog sitting out in the open during broad daylight, or if it is injured, sick or distressed, take it as soon as possible to your local wildlife rescue centre, where they will know how to look after it properly. Alternatively, call the British Hedgehog Preservation Society helpline — 01584 890801 — who will tell you what to do.

An average hedgehog has between 5,000 and 7,000 individual spines. They can eat 200 grams of slugs and other harmful creatures in a single night — between one-fifth and one-third of their body weight. Other names for the hedgehog include urchin, hedge-pig and furze-pig.

Trap small mammals

Although birds are the most visible wild creatures, small mammals are just as common. Indeed, the 75 million or so field voles in Britain actually outnumber us human inhabitants — the only native mammal to do so.

But if that's the case, why do we hardly ever see them? One reason is that many are nocturnal. Another is that small mammals such as mice and voles are eaten by all sorts of other creatures, from owls and kestrels to stoats and foxes. So they sensibly stay out of sight — which means we have to use special methods to see them: small-mammal traps.

Small-mammal traps shouldn't really be used unless you're trained to do so, and experienced at handling whatever you catch. You also need a special licence to handle some creatures, such as the dormouse. So the best way to experience mammal trapping is to go along with an expert, who can show you the tricks of the trade without causing the animals any harm.

Many wildlife trusts and local mammal groups run mammal-trapping events from spring through summer to autumn. They use specially baited traps which attract the animal and keep it fed while it is waiting for the trapper to release it. They are also filled with bedding material so the animal can keep warm.

Traps should be checked frequently, as it is important that the animal is not left there for more than a few hours at most.

Go on a nut hunt

Because small mammals such as voles, wood mice and dormice are so frustratingly hard to see, sometimes you have to turn nature detective. Fortunately you can discover a fair amount just by looking for what they've eaten — in a nut hunt.

Each particular rodent eats nuts in a particular way. So if you find a hazelnut, check whether it shows any of the following features:

* A small, round, neat hole with smooth edges and neat tooth marks — dormouse.
* A small, round hole with rougher edges — wood mouse.
* Crushed to bits! — grey squirrel.

The name 'dormouse' comes from the French word 'dormer' meaning sleep — because this is the only British rodent which hibernates during the autumn and winter. It has been calculated that a dormouse spends about three-quarters of its life asleep!

Watch deer rutting

The annual deer rut — when the dominant males defend their harem of females against rival stags and bucks — is one of Britain's great natural spectacles. Watching a red deer stag bellowing at another, before engaging in head-to-head combat with those

How to identify ...
deer

Our two native species, roe and red deer, have been joined over the centuries by five species introduced from abroad: one (fallow) by the Romans; another (reindeer) in a single herd in the Scottish Highlands; and the other three being brought here in the nineteenth century from Asia.

   Being large and sociable animals, most deer are easier to see than our other mammal species, especially the large herds in deer parks around the country. Even so, it takes practice to tell them apart, as they can be very variable in colour and appearance. The two smallest deer species, muntjac and Chinese water deer, are less sociable and more elusive.

How to identify ...
deer

Red Deer
Our largest land mammal: males are magnificent beasts, especially in the autumn rutting season when they use their huge antlers to fight off rival males and win the female. Most common in Scotland, but also found in hilly regions of England, as well as in some parks and the grounds of stately homes.

Fallow Deer
Introduced here by the Romans, this elegant deer is one of our most attractive mammals. Look out for the white-spotted coat and the male's distinctive flattened antlers. Fallow deer are most common in southern Britain, especially in herds in parks.

Roe Deer
Our other native deer is on the increase, and can often be seen in singles, pairs or small family groups, especially in Scotland, northern England and the south-west. Uniform brown in colour with distinctive twin horns on the male's head.

Muntjac

Our smallest deer, and much more doglike in size, shape and general appearance than any other British deer. Often seen running away, revealing a whitish tail like a rabbit or hare. Has become much commoner in recent years, and can be seen throughout southern and eastern England.

Sika Deer

About the size of a fallow deer, but with the markings and general appearance of the larger red deer, including quite large antlers. Will also sometimes cross-breed with the reds. Has thicker neck and whiter rear than other deer. Found scattered across parts of Britain, especially Scotland.

Reindeer

This unmistakable creature, always associated with Father Christmas, can be seen in a free-living feral herd on the Cairngorms in Scotland. Visit in winter to see these beautiful animals in the snow.

Chinese Water Deer

Our rarest and most elusive deer, found only in the East Anglian broads and fens. Larger than a muntjac, with bizarre tusks used by males and females in courtship.

clashing antlers, is an unforgettable experience. It's also surprisingly easy to see — provided you get the timing right.

Where to go

For genuinely wild deer, you need to venture into Britain's wild places, such as Exmoor, the Scottish Highlands and the New Forest — though in such vast areas it's not difficult to miss the spectacle.

So a good compromise is to visit a deer park, where herds of 'semi-wild' deer roam free. Richmond Park on the outskirts of south-west London, Tatton Park in Cheshire and Fountains Abbey in Yorkshire are ideal.

When to go

* The red deer rut usually occurs from late September into October, though the exact time will vary depending on the location and the weather conditions that particular year.
* The fallow deer rut happens slightly later, usually from the middle of October through to November.
* Early mornings and evenings are the best times, as not only are the deer more active but the light is usually better.
* Fine, cold days also generally see more activity, and are better conditions for watching the rut.

Tips

* To find rutting deer, listen and smell as well as look. Listen for their roaring sounds; look out for areas where the deer have scraped the ground; and see if you can smell the distinctive scent they give out at this time of year.
* Be quiet, and move slowly and carefully — you don't want to frighten the animals you've come to see.

* Don't go too close — a rutting stag can and will attack. If you are confronted by a stag, stay very still and quiet — he will probably decide you're not a threat and walk away.
* If you're looking for truly wild deer, wear camouflaged clothing and put mud on your face as they are very wary.

A stag's antlers are measured by counting the number of individual horns, known as 'points'. A Red Deer stag with 12 or more points is known as a 'royal stag', but fossil antlers have been discovered with as many as 22 points.

Make a nest box

Making a nest box isn't as difficult as you might think. You don't need to be an expert carpenter — all you need is some wood, the right tools, and a bit of persistence.

Basic tools and equipment you will need

* A plank of wood, about one to 1—1.5 metres long, 15—20cm wide, and about 15—20mm thick.
* A sharp wood saw.
* Galvanised nails, panel pins or wood screws.
* A strip of leather, rubber or heavy-duty carpet tape which you need to hinge the lid.
* A hook and eye to make the lid secure from predators.
* A power drill, with a suitably-sized cutting blade for making the entrance hole.
* A tape measure.

1. Mark out the plank with the shape and dimensions of your box. The back panel can vary in size, depending on where you want to fix it, but must be at least 250mm long.

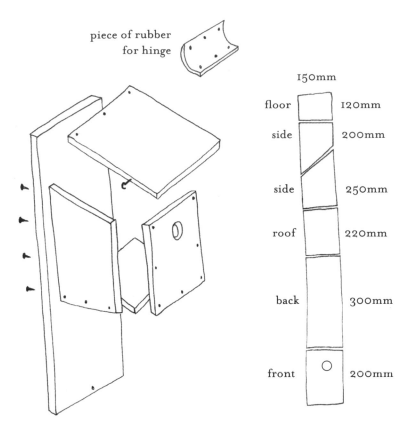

piece of rubber
for hinge

150mm

floor   120mm

side   200mm

side   250mm

roof   220mm

back   300mm

front   200mm

1. Cut the wood into six pieces, being careful to keep the cuts straight and at right angles to the edge of the plank. The exception to this is the cut between the two side pieces, which should be made at a shallow angle.

2. Drill two small holes at the top and bottom of the back panel, so that once you've finished making the box you'll be able to fix it to a fence, wall or tree.

3. Nail or screw the two side panels to the base.

4. Drill a hole in the front panel, about 125mm from the bottom. The hole can vary in size from 25mm for smaller tits such as blue and coal tits, to 28mm for great tits, and 32mm for house sparrows.

5. Drill a few small holes in the base so that water can drain away if the box gets flooded in heavy rain.

6. Nail or screw the base and front panel to the box.

7. Fix the roof, using a strip of leather, rubber or carpet tape to make a hinge. Make the lid secure with a hook and eye.

8. Before you put your box up, waterproof the outside with a wood-preserving agent such as creosote (or one of the branded wood preservers like Cuprinol or Fenceguard). Never put this on the inside of the box, as this may harm the birds.

Don't worry if your box looks a bit wonky, or doesn't match up to the ones in the shop. Remember that natural nest sites in walls and trees don't come in a regular shape or size, yet the birds are still happy to use them.

Putting up your nest box

When you're deciding where to put your nest box, there are a few basic rules to follow.

* Put your box up in autumn or winter, so the birds have a chance to get used to it before the breeding season begins.
* Put it up on a tree, wall or garden fence, at least 1.5 metres above the ground. Use large nails or screws if you're fixing it to a post or fence; or hang from a wire if you're attaching it to a tree.
* Make sure the box faces away from direct sunlight, preferably somewhere between north and south-east.
* Try to tilt the front of the box downwards a little, to keep out the rain.
* If you're putting up several nest boxes, keep them some distance apart, to stop rival males fighting each other over disputed territory.

Once your box is up, be patient. Garden birds often take a while to get used to a nest box, and you may have to wait a whole year before they venture inside and make it their home. And when they do, try not to check it out too often — it may disturb the birds and cause them to desert their eggs.

Finally, every autumn, when you are absolutely sure all the young have left the box, it's time for a good clean-out. Throw away any old nesting material, and then give it a thorough scrub using hot water and washing-up liquid. Don't use household chemicals as it may harm the birds which occupy it next year.

Every February, the British Trust for Ornithology organises National Nest Box Week, to encourage more people to provide nest boxes for their garden birds. (See *Useful Addresses* for details.)

The pair of blue tits in your nest box will be kept pretty busy by their hungry young. In the spring, during the two or three weeks the baby birds are in the nest, their parents will bring back as many as 12,000 caterpillars to feed them.

Dig a pond in your garden

It has been said that a wildlife garden without a pond is like a theatre without a stage. And it's certainly true that even the smallest pond will add a new dimension to your garden's attractiveness to wildlife.

By providing somewhere for birds and mammals to drink and bathe, for amphibians and insects to lay their eggs, and for flowers and aquatic plants to grow, you'll also be able to enjoy watching a whole new world of wild creatures.

What you need

* Bamboo poles or rope to mark out the shape of your pond.
* Spades to dig out the soil, and a wheelbarrow to take it away.
* A tape measure and calculator to work out what size lining you will need.
* Old blankets or carpet to protect the lining against sharp objects.
* Butyl rubber lining – you can get this from specialist aquatic suppliers or your local garden centre.

* A sharp knife or heavy-duty scissors.
* Stones or rocks to keep the lining in place.
* Sand to cover the lining.

What to do

* Before you start digging, plan the size and shape of your pond and mark this out using bamboo poles or a length of rope.
* Then, starting from the middle, dig your hole.
* Make sure you vary the depth to provide shallow and deep areas — between 30cm and 80cm deep is ideal (once the lining etc. are in this will make a pond between 10cm and 60cm deep).
* Remove any sharp rocks and stones and add a layer of sand.
* Put the old blankets or carpets on top of the sand, then the lining on top of those.
* Put in another layer of sand.
* Fill the pond with a garden hose; then add a bucketful of water from another pond.
* Your pond is ready to go …

It may not look like much, but if you add some aquatic plants (ask at your local suppliers for advice on which ones) it will start to take shape. Ideally you want a combination of submerged, floating and edge-based plants — water milfoil, water lilies, yellow iris and reed mace are ideal.

Top tips

* Don't put in fish. Fishponds and wildlife ponds don't really go together as the fish tend to eat the wildlife.
* Don't take plants from the wild.
* Keep the surface of your pond tidy, removing leaves in autumn and algae in summer.
* If young children (four years old and below) visit the garden, then make sure the pond is securely covered so they can't fall in.

Plant a native hedgerow in your garden

A hedgerow made up of native plants is one of the best ways to provide food and shelter for a whole range of garden creatures. A hedgerow is easy to plant and will provide a refuge for wildlife — as well as an attractive feature for your garden — in just a couple of years.

When to plant

The best time to plant your hedge is during the winter, between November and March, when hedgerow plants are dormant. Don't go ahead when the ground is waterlogged or there's a heavy frost, as this may kill off your plants before they have a chance to grow.

What to plant

Choose native species of hedgerow plant, such as hawthorn and blackthorn (which together should make up the majority of your hedgerow), hazel, dogwood, field maple, dog rose, field rose, guelder rose and alder buckthorn. These are available from specialist nurseries or mail-order suppliers, who will also be able to give you advice on when and how to plant your hedge.

How to plant

* Decide where you want to put the hedgerow, and clear all weeds from the soil to a width of about one metre, and to the length you want the hedgerow to be.
* Spread a layer of compost or rotted manure across the area to a depth of about 5cm.
* Plant two rows of 3–4 plants each per metre, about 30–50cm apart, staggering the plants along each row.

How to identify ...
hedgerow plants

It is said that you can tell the age of a hedgerow by counting the number of different kinds of woody plants it contains — one for every century of its life. That may or may not be true, but it is certainly possible to count at least a dozen trees, shrubs and wild flowers in or alongside many hedgerows.

Take along a couple of field guides — one for trees and another for wild flowers — to help you. Here are a few common ones to look out for.

How to identify ...
hedgerow plants

Blackthorn
Similar to hawthorn, but a good way to tell the two apart is that the blackthorn's white blossom comes out before the leaves instead of afterwards. In the autumn produces hard purplish-black fruit known as sloes.

Hawthorn
With its white fluffy flowers in bloom from late April or May onwards, this is one of our commonest hedgerow plants. Later in the year has bunches of bright red berries.

Elder
The MDF of the plant world – tough, flexible and very fast-growing. The creamy blossoms fill the air with scent in May and June, while the purplish berries hang from the shrub's branches in August and September.

Hazel
Commonly planted for its tasty and nutritious nuts, which are plundered by all sorts of animals including the scarce dormouse. Often found in ancient hedgerows along parish boundaries.

Holly
The red berries of holly appear in early winter, so its prickly evergreen sprigs have long been associated with pagan festivals and also with Christmas.

Bramble
One of the commonest hedgerow plants, whose juicy purple fruit is welcomed by birds, mammals and people alike.

Guelder rose
A small, scrubby native plant often found in mixed hedgerows; with white flowers in spring and red berries in autumn.

Ash
Like the oak, ash trees are often found in ancient hedgerows which originated in woodland.

Oak
Oak trees are often found along hedgerows, indicating that the hedge itself may have originally been part of a larger woodland.

Field maple
A common hedgerow tree which is often coppiced to keep its height down. An important food plant for butterflies and moths.

Spindle
This often overlooked hedgerow plant produces small pinkish-red berries in autumn which although poisonous to humans are loved by birds — especially robins.

Sycamore
This non-native tree often crops up in hedgerows, thanks to its ability to grow in almost any kind of soil.

Rowan
Also known as the mountain ash, because of its liking for higher ground, the rowan produces orange-red berries which can be used to make jelly, and are a favourite food of many birds.

Hornbeam
This native tree is mainly found in southern and eastern England, preferring dryer soils.

Willow
Especially on damper ground willow trees are often pollarded to create field boundaries that act as substitute hedges. Used to make all sorts of things including baskets and cricket bats.

* Add another thick layer of mulch.
* Once your hedgerow is in, try to keep the area around it free from weeds to allow the plants to grow.
* If you have animals such as pets or rabbits which might eat the hedge, protect it with wire or fencing, especially in the first couple of years when the young plants are most vulnerable.

Since the end of the Second World War we have lost over one-third of our native hedgerows — enough to stretch around the world more than five times.

Be blown by the wind

When the wind blows really hard — especially during autumn gales — find an exposed spot on a high hill and just allow yourself to be blown around by its mighty force. Wonderful!

Autumn weather lore

No warmth, no cheerfulness, no healthful ease,
No comfortable feel in any member,
No shade, no shine, no butterflies, no bees,
No fruits, no flowers, no leaves, no birds,
No-vember.
THOMAS HOOD

Autumn can be a pretty miserable time of year, weather-wise, as Thomas Hood's poem suggests. And it has also given rise to all sorts of verses, proverbs and old wives' tales about the weather, many of which come from our observations of nature.

Many suggest that wild creatures somehow know when the coming winter will be a hard one, and make sure they get enough to eat to see them through the cold spell: 'When birds and badgers are fat in October, expect a cold winter.'

But if the snow and ice has arrived as early as November, it was believed that the coming winter would be a mild one: 'If there's ice in November that will bear a duck, there'll be nothing after but sludge and muck.'

Mist or fog, on the other hand, is good news — especially early on an autumn morning, meaning fine weather to come that day.

You can also observe the behaviour of familiar wild animals and use this to predict the weather, as in the following beliefs.

* When rooks 'tumble' in the air, doing amazing acrobatics as if for fun, it is widely believed that bad weather is on the way — almost as if the birds are enjoying themselves while they can.
* If you have a hedgehog in your garden, he will make a den at this time of year in preparation for the coming winter. Hedgehogs make two entrance holes to their den, one at the north and one at the south; and as bad weather approaches from one or other direction he will block up the hole to stop the rain and wind getting inside.
* If geese or other waterbirds are seen heading out to sea, fine weather is meant to be on the way; but if they head inland, bad weather is due.

Winter

I love to see the old heaths withered brake
Mingle its crimpled leaves with furze and ling
While the old heron from the lonely lake
Starts slow and flaps his melancholy wing
And oddling crow in idle motions swing
On the half rotten ash trees topmost twig …
And coy bumbarrels twenty in a drove
Flit down the hedgerows in the frozen plain
And hang on little twigs and start again.

JOHN CLARE

Of all the seasons, winter may seem the least promising — at least when it comes to being out and about with nature. Surely it's better to stay indoors, open our Christmas presents, and wait until the coming of spring?

On the other hand, after too much food and drink during the festive season, it's always good to wrap up warm and go out for a walk — a great way to clear away the cobwebs and breathe in some fresh air.

And although things are quieter in winter from a wildlife point of view, there are still things to see and do — provided you know where to look. Woodlands may seem empty, but with patience you can hear the high-pitched calls of flocks of small birds in search of food.

Beaches are great places for a winter walk too — and if you feel really tough, why not have a swim in the sea? — it's warmer than you might think! If you head for open water — either inland or on the coast — there should be large flocks of wildfowl and wading birds which spend the winter in Britain because of our mild climate.

Talking of climate, it's obvious that in recent years things have changed. We no longer get the hard winters we used to, with long periods of ice and snow — in fact, in many parts of southern and western Britain we hardly get snow at all these days. Although that means we may not be able to build a snowman or have snowball fights like we used to, it may instead bring new opportunities to see winter wildlife.

For example, more kinds of butterflies are spending the winter in Britain nowadays, while other insects are emerging on mild winter days. So even in January and February, a fair, sunny day can bring sightings of bumblebees and butterflies on the wing — a sure sign that spring is round the corner.

Feed the ducks

Is there anyone who hasn't fed the ducks at least once in their lives? Hopefully we'll carry on doing so, even though some local councils have forbidden this fun activity on the grounds that it might harm the birds, or attract rats. So at the risk of encouraging you to break the law, here are a few tips on what to do.

✳ Although white bread doesn't do ducks much good, it won't do them any real harm either. So if that's what you've got, use it.
✳ Wholemeal bread, stale buns, bits of fruit, etc. are also fine, and will be gobbled up not just by the ducks, but by any passing geese, swans, coots and moorhens, and those aerial acrobats above the park pond – gulls.
✳ If you want to feed the ducks regularly, and are prepared to spend a bit more to give them something more nutritious, then buy seeds or grains from a reputable bird-food supplier.
✳ Try to feed the smallest and weediest birds you can see – so avoid the Canada geese and mute swans, and instead sidle up to that shy little moorhen.

How to identify ...
ducks and other waterbirds

We all love feeding the ducks, and it's another way to get to know a range of different birds. Your local park pond is a good place to start; or visit a river or lake — any large area of water will be home to a good range of the birds featured here.

Most ducks come in two plumages: male and female. The male is usually brightly coloured, and the female duller — because she does all the incubating duties, and needs to be camouflaged to avoid being seen by a hungry fox.

But ducks aren't the only waterbirds you're likely to see. Swans and geese are pretty obvious, but what about those little black birds with the white bill, or that one with red on its beak and a white streak along its side? Not ducks, but coot and moorhen, members of the rail family. Other waterbirds you may see are grebes, herons and — in much of southern Britain — egrets. If you're really lucky, a kingfisher may even flash past ...

By the way, park ponds and lakes are often home to exotic, introduced wildfowl which may not be featured in your bird book. If you're not sure what bird you're looking at, take a photo and then check it out when you're back at home using a more comprehensive bird book or the Internet.

How to identify ...
ducks and
other waterbirds

Shoveler
Male has bright green head, white breast and chestnut sides — and that huge, spoon-shaped bill which it uses to filter tiny items of food from the water. Female speckled brown like mallard, but also has huge bill.

Mallard
The classic duck — male has bottle-green head, magenta breast and white collar; female speckled brown with purplish patch on the wing. Both have yellow bills. Beware domesticated duck breeds, originally descended from mallards, that come in all shapes, sizes and colours.

Wigeon
The male is a really handsome duck: mainly grey, but with a chestnut head, creamy forehead and black under the tail. Female deep chestnut brown. Both have short, stubby bills for grazing on grass.

Gadwall
Male is subtle shades of grey, black and brown; female like female mallard but smaller. Both have small white patch on wings.

Pochard
Male has chestnut head, black breast and grey body; the female is duller and greyer, with brown head. Dives for food.

Tufted Duck
Male black with contrasting white sides, and with little black tuft on the back of his head. Female dark brown with paler sides and smaller tuft. Dives for food.

Coot
All black, apart from prominent white bill and white forehead. Larger than closely related moorhen. Chicks have red on head — easily confused with baby moorhens. Dives for food.

Great Crested Grebe

Slim, elegant bird, often seen diving for food. In spring and summer has beautiful orange and brown crests on either side of its head. In winter plainer, with white front and brown back.

Moorhen

Smaller and more slender than coot, and more colourful: with purplish-brown plumage, a jagged pale line along the sides and white under the tail. Most obvious difference from coot is the red and yellow bill.

Little Grebe or Dabchick

Tiny little bird, looking a bit like a baby duck. Fluffy rear end and short, sharp bill. In summer has chestnut patches on face.

Mute Swan

Our largest bird — elegant, serene and unmistakable. Males have slightly larger 'knob' on top of their orange bill.

Canada Goose

Big, noisy quarrelsome bird. Mainly brown, with dark neck and head and obvious white patch under the chin.

Grey Heron

Tall, slender bird with very long legs. Basically grey above and white below, with black on head and down front. Long, pointed yellow bill, ideal for spearing fish. Shy, and often seen in flight — looks huge on bowed wings.

Little Egret

Beautiful white creature — smaller than heron but similar shape and posture. Once very rare, but now doing well in southern Britain, and spreading northwards.

Kingfisher

Stunning jewel of a bird: electric blue above, deep orange below, with a dagger-like bill. Much smaller than you might think — only just bigger than a sparrow.

* For a real show, throw small bits of bread up into the air and watch the gulls swoop down and catch a piece before it hits the water. You can play a game with your friends and family — who can get the highest number of catches with ten pieces of bread?

Coots and moorhens may look like ducks, act like ducks, and even sound a bit like ducks, but they're not related at all. They're actually members of the rail family which have adapted to life on the water. Next time you see one, take a look at their bills (short and pointed rather than long and flat) and their feet (long toes with tiny webs rather than fully webbed), and you'll see the difference.

Go pishing to attract small birds

Yes, that's right — go pishing. It may sound rude, and you may get some funny looks doing it, but it's the best way I know to get really up-close-and-personal with some of our smallest birds.

You start by visiting a local park, wood or hedgerow on an autumn or winter's day — generally the coldest days are best.

Listen out for tiny, high-pitched noises — the calls made by tits and goldcrests as they try to keep in contact with each other. At this time of year, they tend to travel in flocks — it's the best way to find food and avoid danger. The more pairs of eyes, the more food they can find, and the more likely they are to spot a predator and sound the alarm.

When you've heard the sounds, follow them until they get loud enough to hear quite clearly. Then stand still, and make a loud 'pish-pish-pish' sound, repeating yourself and making sure the 'shhhhh' really sounds hissy.

At this point, you may start to feel a bit silly, especially if anyone's watching you. But bear with me — it really does work. If you keep on pishing, eventually the birds will start to get curious, and come to investigate.

After a minute or two, you'll notice a movement in the leaves in front of you, and a tiny bird will pop out. If you keep pishing he'll usually stay still for a moment or two, probably wondering why this huge, strange-looking creature (you) is making such a peculiar noise. He may even be joined by a few of his fellows.

As you watch them, think about the lives these little birds lead. Every day a blue tit or goldcrest must eat about one-quarter of its own body weight — just to survive. So once you've had a good look at them, let them carry on their way — they've got work to do.

The theory behind pishing is that the birds think you're another bird which has found a predator (perhaps an owl or a hawk) and is seeing it off. Oddly, instead of flying away, they come to check out the threat for themselves. Well, they do have very tiny brains ...

The tiny yet pugnacious goldcrest is Britain's smallest songbird — just nine centimetres long and weighing about five grams — about the same as a twenty-pence coin.

Search for hibernating butterflies

Butterflies in winter? Surely that can't be right. Well, yes, it's true that almost all of Britain's different kinds of butterfly either head away from our shores for the winter, or spend the cold weather as caterpillars or in their pupa stage.

But several kinds — including the small tortoiseshell, peacock, red admiral, comma and brimstone — spend the winter hibernating, as adults.

The easiest of these to find is the small tortoiseshell, as they seek out quiet, sheltered places — so look for them in your garage, garden shed or, if you have one, outside toilet.

They can be tricky to spot — they rest with their wings closed, so the bright colours don't usually show. Look out for them high up, where the wall meets the ceiling, or perhaps in a corner of a room.

If you do find a hibernating butterfly make sure you don't disturb it — if they wake up too early, when the weather is still cold, they will lose valuable energy and may not be able to survive the rest of the winter.

The colour in a butterfly's wings is not always what it seems. Some butterflies reflect light in a way that produces new colours — known as iridescence — which can only be seen from a certain angle.

Go beachcombing along the tideline

One of the most satisfying and enjoyable things you can do along our coasts is to go beachcombing: taking a walk along the tideline to see what you can find. Of course you can do this at any time of year, but there's something special about being out in the middle of winter, when the summer-holiday crowds have long gone, and the beach is deserted.

Almost anything found at sea can eventually wash up on the tideline, and over the course of time, much of it does. This may be natural objects such as seashells, the bodies of dead birds or other sea creatures, or man-made objects such as remains from a shipwreck – or, more likely nowadays, the ever increasing mountain of rubbish that gets dumped at sea.

So although you may occasionally come across something you would rather not see, beachcombing is endlessly unpredictable and fascinating, as you really do never know quite what you'll come across, even if you walk along the same stretch of tideline every day of your life.

The best time to go beachcombing is on a falling tide, as the seas reveal their secrets. Every tide brings new objects – the 'flotsam and jetsam' of the modern world. Flotsam and jetsam are used interchangeably to describe anything washed up on the beach – although strictly speaking flotsam is any object that floats (e.g. something washed off a ship or shipwreck), while jetsam is an object that has been deliberately thrown overboard by the crew of a boat or ship.

Below are some natural objects to look out for and collect.

* Pebbles: everything from rounded ones made smooth by aeons of being beaten by the waves, to sharp, jagged lumps of rock recently broken off the cliffs by autumn gales.
* Sea shells: from common-or-garden cockles, mussels, winkles and whelks, to the more exotic-looking razor shells and scallops.
* Cuttlefish bones: glowing white among the sand or shingle, these are also a common find, as are 'mermaid's purses', the egg cases of the ray or dogfish (a relative of the shark).
* Seaweed: great strands of kelp, some many metres long; or bladder-wrack, a brownish-green seaweed usually found on rocks, whose air chambers make a satisfying sound when you squeeze them between your finger and thumb until they pop.
* Fossils: depending where you are in the country, there's a good chance of finding ancient fossils – some of them many tens, even hundreds, of millions of years old.

- Driftwood: not strictly natural, as it may well be a piece of decking or other wood from a ship. But the effect of the sea will often create a really beautiful object you can take home and use as the basis for a work of art.
- Semi-precious stones: lumps of amber (fossilised pine resin about 40 million years old), or smaller, colourful gems.
- Live creatures: stranded jellyfish are common, especially after winter storms.

Some tips

- Don't go beachcombing on a rising tide – you may get cut off as the water comes up the beach.
- Wear shoes with grips such as trainers or walking boots – rocks can be very slippery.
- Turn over rocks to look for what's underneath; but make sure you put the rock back in the same place afterwards.
- Check out the tideline itself, as well as rock pools.
- Dig down into the sand to see what you can find.
- Take a bucket which you can fill with seawater to look at any living creatures you find.
- Once you've finished looking, put live creatures back where you found them – the next tide will usually wash them back to sea.
- Be careful near the underside of cliffs – rocks frequently fall, especially in winter.

The British Isles has more than 15,000 kilometres of coastline, and over 6,000 different islands.

Watch the sun rise and set
on the same day

A survey in Japan (the land of the rising sun) found that over half the nation's children had never seen the sun rise or set. Yet this is a great way to get to understand the daily rhythms of the universe – and it has the added advantage that you can do it almost anywhere.

Choose a day in the middle of winter, when you won't have to get up too early or go to bed too late. Check the weather forecast the day before – you'll need high pressure with clear skies, so you can be sure the sun's rays will get through.

Pick a place with a bit of height – a local hill is ideal. Check out the sunrise and sunset times using a diary or the Internet, and make sure you get up early enough to be in place a few minutes before the sun comes over the horizon. Wrap up warm, take some food and drink, and wait for the first rays to appear.

In the evening, go back to the same place – but remember that the sun sets in the opposite half of the sky; rising in the east and setting in the west. What you've just witnessed is the turning of the Earth, which rotates through a full cycle every twenty-four hours, and gives us day and night.

The sun is about 93 million miles away from the Earth; but the moon is only about 250,000 miles away. Yet to us, they usually appear roughly the same size. This amazing coincidence is because the sun is roughly 360 times further away than the moon, and also about 400 times the size.

Visit a starling roost at dusk

As a child I remember seeing the starlings coming in to roost at London's Leicester Square on a chilly winter's night. I can still recall the incredible noise – a constant chattering and whistling, as if the birds were talking to each other. Nowadays, sadly, the London roost has all but vanished, and there are only a few gatherings left in the country – the largest is near my home on the Somerset Levels.

Starlings are one of those birds we take for granted – or at least we used to until their numbers started to fall dramatically. Thanks to television wildlife programmes featuring their incredible roosts, we now appreciate them more than we did.

A big starling roost is one of nature's great spectacles. Watching hundreds of thousands – sometimes even millions – of these birds twisting and turning in the air is an unforgettable experience, so go and see it while you still can.

There are two reasons why many roosts have disappeared. First, the starling population has dropped by well over half in the past thirty years or so, possibly as a result of intensive farming, which uses pesticides to kill off the tiny creatures on which the starling feeds. Second, milder winters in Russia (almost certainly because of global warming) have vastly reduced the number of birds heading westwards to Britain to spend the winter here.

Even so, the famous roost on the Somerset Levels can still contain well over a million birds – the most you are ever likely to see of any species, anywhere. To find out about starling roosts check out websites and local information lines which give up-to-date information on numbers and exact locations.

Why do starlings roost in such large numbers?

* Safety in numbers: all birds have to sleep sometimes – and when they do, they make themselves vulnerable to being attacked by predators such as birds of prey or foxes. So by getting together in huge groups each individual bird reduces the chances of being killed and eaten.
* Keeping warm: being together also helps birds retain body heat, especially during very cold winter nights when the temperature may drop well below zero.

* Exchanging information: hearing the noise made by millions of starlings as they settle down for the night, we might assume that they are 'talking to each other'. In fact, it's thought that the hungriest birds seek out the healthiest looking ones, which have had a good day's feeding. The next morning they follow them to their feeding grounds, taking advantage of their knowledge.

Go swimming in the sea in winter

The seas around Britain are warmer in December than on May Day. This is a result of the fact that although the sea warms up more slowly than the land in spring and summer, it also cools down more slowly. So even on Christmas Day the sea temperature may be higher than you think.

Another advantage of swimming in winter is that because the air temperature is cooler, the sea will seem warmer — think about how cold it feels when you plunge into the waves on a hot summer's day and you'll see what I mean.

Founded by a group of Victorian gentlemen in 1860, Brighton Swimming Club holds an annual Christmas Day swim by the Palace Pier, in which dozens of swimmers put on fancy dress and take the plunge as their family and friends look on.

Go and look for winter wildlife

Although we think of spring and summer as the best times to look for wildlife, there's plenty of activity in winter as well — you just need to know where to look. And there are some creatures which may be easier to see in this season than at any other time

of year – though you will have to travel north to the Scottish Highlands to have the best chance.

- Mountain hare: found only in the Highlands of Scotland, on some Scottish islands, and in the Peak District in central England. Changes its appearance through the seasons, and in winter turns almost completely white, to hide from predators like golden eagles.
- Stoat: another animal whose fur turns white in winter (apart from the black tip of its tail). Always hard to spot, but the short winter days leave little time for hunting so they do become more visible at this time of year.
- Reindeer: Santa's favourite animal went extinct in Britain about 8,000 years ago, but a small herd was reintroduced to the Cairngorms in Scotland in the 1950s. There are now about 150 of these magnificent beasts, which can be seen wandering over the high tops of the mountains, where they are perfectly adapted to the harsh winter climate.

Take part in a bird survey

Britain's birdlife has been watched, studied and surveyed more than any other group of birds anywhere in the world – and as a result we know a tremendous amount about familiar birds such as the song thrush, robin and house sparrow. Interestingly, most of what we know wasn't discovered by professional scientists, but by ordinary birdwatchers. And you can contribute to increasing this sum of knowledge – and help our birds as a result – even if you're a complete beginner.

There are three surveys you can take part in: two of them take place once a year, and take just an hour to do; the other is something you can do all year round.

1. The RSPB Big Garden Birdwatch

This takes place every year, on the fourth weekend of January, and has now been going for more than twenty-five years. During that time millions of people have taken part — with about half a million having a go every year.

All you have to do is watch the birds in your garden for an hour, any time over the course of the weekend, and count the maximum number of each species you see. Then you can send in your sightings either using a paper form or on the RSPB's website.

The results from all over the country are collected together and then published in the spring. The top five in 2008 were house sparrow, starling, blackbird, blue tit, and chaffinch.

2. The RSPB Big Schools Birdwatch

This is the same as the Big Garden Birdwatch, except this time schoolchildren count the birds they see in their school grounds. More than 30,000 schoolchildren up and down the country take part in January and February every year, and there are free information packs, posters and other goodies available to teachers. The top five birds in our playgrounds are: starling, blackbird, black-headed gull, wood pigeon and house sparrow.

3. The BTO Garden BirdWatch

This survey, run by the British Trust for Ornithology, is a great way for you to help our garden birds by helping us learn more about them. By counting the birds all year round we can see when numbers go up and down as bird populations change — and it's good fun too. People who take part also get a regular magazine updating them on national results.

(See end of book for further details on how to contact the RSPB and BTO.)

Six things to do when it snows

Despite global warming, it does still snow in Britain — indeed, if you live in Scotland, Northern Ireland or the north of England it's a rare winter that passes without at least one snowfall. And even if you live in the relatively snow-free south, you should always be prepared for that unexpected appearance of white stuff falling from the sky.

1. Make a snowman

* Start by rolling the snow into a large snowball — at least a metre across if you can manage it. Keep patting the snow as you roll it, to pack it in as densely as possible. This will be the main 'body' of your snowman.
* Then roll some more snow into a slightly smaller ball — about 50cm across — this will form the upper body.
* Finally make a third, even smaller, ball — this time about 20–30cm across — for the snowman's head.
* Put the medium-sized ball on top of the large one, pushing down firmly to stick the two together (but not so hard that the whole thing collapses). Then place the smallest ball firmly on top of the other two.
* Take two pieces of dark stone, pebbles or coins (in my day we used coal but you might find that a bit hard to get hold of) and push them into the head to make the eyes.
* Push a carrot into the head below the 'eyes' to make the nose.
* Put more small stones or pebbles in a semicircle beneath the carrot to make the snowman's mouth.
* Give him a hat and wrap a scarf around his neck to keep him nice and warm.

And do it all as quickly as you can before the snow starts to melt.

2. Catch a snowflake on your tongue

There can be few experiences more pure and simple than opening your mouth when it's snowing and allowing the snowflakes to fall upon your tongue.

3. Look at a snowflake through a magnifying glass

It's often said that no two snowflakes are alike, and while this is technically correct at the microscopic level, to the naked eye many snowflakes do look remarkably similar. But if you look really closely at snowflakes through a magnifying glass you will begin to see the complex, beautiful patterns of these six-sided crystals of ice.

4. Make snow angels

This is fun to do – provided you're dressed warmly, ideally in waterproof clothing so you don't get soaked.

* Find a nice, even patch of pure, white snow, which people and dogs haven't discovered yet.
* Lie flat on your back, as carefully as you can, trying not to disturb the snow around your body.
* Slowly stretch out your arms and legs – then move your arms up and down across the snow in an arc from your waist to almost (but not quite) above your head; and move your legs in and out from straight down to stretched out as far as you can.
* Get up, again as carefully as you can, and step back. There, on the snow, is your very own 'snow angel'.

5. Slide down a slope on a tray or bin liner

Sledging and tobogganing are great activities — but how many people nowadays spend good money on buying a sledge on the off chance that one day they might be able to use it?

So if it does snow, and you want to go tobogganing, you need something to use instead. You could try:

* A large wooden or plastic tray.
* A plastic bin liner — the thick garden refuse sacks are the best as the thin ones are likely to rip.
* A large cardboard box — folded flat and taped up with any strong sticky tape.

And, of course …

6. Have a snowball fight

* Roll up some snow, pressing it as hard as you can to pack it together into a ball.
* Throw it at your friend/brother/sister/mum/dad/grandson/ daughter/boss/the postman* (*tick as appropriate).
* Run or duck!

A haiku about snow

*The snow is melting
and the village is flooded
with children.*
KOBAYASHI ISSA

Winter weather lore

Watching the behaviour of wildlife in winter is a really good way to predict the weather – at least for the next day or two. Birds, in particular, will move south and west in large numbers to avoid a sudden spell of very cold weather, as snow and ice makes it difficult for them to find food.

So watch out for large flocks of birds flying overhead – particularly lapwings, which are especially vulnerable to harsh weather; and redwings, our smallest thrush, which also struggle to survive in snowy conditions. Geese and ducks will also often move ahead of a fall of snow; though as long as the water they feed on remains ice-free they will often stay put, as they're still able to feed.

We don't get really hard winters any more, but in the past these had a devastating effect on our birdlife. Back in 1962–63, when the 'Big Freeze' cloaked much of Britain in white for more than three months, birds like kingfishers had nowhere to go and as a result many died.

The Dartford warbler, one of our rarest breeding birds, dropped to just a dozen pairs; though the long run of mild winters since then has allowed numbers to recover very well.

Nowadays, with such mild winters, birds face another problem: many are fooled into nesting too early — sometimes even before Christmas. The trouble is that when the young hatch there may be a further cold spell, making it hard for the adults to find food, so the chicks die.

The same problem affects insects such as bumblebees and butterflies, and hibernating mammals like hedgehogs, which often emerge on a fine winter's day, only to suffer when the weather turns chilly again.

If the unexpected happens, and we do get a few days of wintry weather, here are some ways you can help our birds and other garden wildlife.

* Keep your bird feeders topped up with high-energy food like sunflower hearts, mixed seeds and fat balls.
* If it does snow, put out food on bird tables and on the ground for birds like the dunnock which don't come to hanging feeders.
* Make sure your bird bath is kept topped up with water. If it's iced over, pour cold (not hot) water into it until the ice melts.
* If you have a garden pond, make a hole in the ice so that birds and other animals can drink.

And finally, as you wait for the primroses to bloom, the butterflies to appear, and the swallows to arrive, a hopeful line from the poet Shelley: 'If winter comes, can spring be far behind?'

Useful Contacts

Natural England
1 East Parade, Sheffield, S1 2ET
Tel: 0114 241 8920
www.naturalengland.org.uk

The National Trust
PO Box 39, Warrington WA5 7WD
Tel: 0844 800 1895
www.nationaltrust.org.uk

The Wildlife Trusts
The Kiln, Waterside, Mather Road, Newark, Nottinghamshire
NG24 1WT
Tel: 0870 036 7711
www.wildlifetrusts.org

RSPB (Royal Society for the Protection of Birds)
The Lodge, Sandy, Beds SG19 2DL
Tel: 01767 680551
www.rspb.org.uk

BTO (British Trust for Ornithology)
The National Centre for Ornithology, The Nunnery, Thetford,
Norfolk IP24 2PU
Tel: 01842 750050
www.bto.org

WWT (Wildfowl and Wetlands Trust)
Slimbridge, Glos GL2 7BT
Tel: 01453 891900
www.wwt.org.uk

Buglife – the Invertebrate Conservation Trust
170A Park Road, Peterborough PE1 2UF
Tel: 01733 201210
www.buglife.org.uk

Butterfly Conservation
Manor Yard, East Lulworth, Wareham, Dorset, BH20 5QP
Tel: 01929 400209
www.butterfly-conservation.org

The Woodland Trust
Autumn Court, Grantham, Lincolnshire NG31 6LL
Tel: 01476 581111
www.woodland-trust.org.uk

BTCV – British Trust for Conservation Volunteers
Sedum House, Mallard Way, Doncaster DN4 8DB
Tel: 01302 388883
www.btcv.org.uk

Further Reading

Here is a selection of the best field guides, books and magazines that will help you make the most of wildlife watching in Britain – at any time of year! Most titles will be obtainable in high street bookshops, or to obtain them by mail order, contact Subbuteo Books www.wildlifebooks.com; or the Natural History Book Service www.nhbs.com

General

How to Watch Wildlife, Oddie, Moss & Pitcher (Collins)
Collins Wild Guides: series includes *Birds*, *Wild Flowers*, *Butterflies*, *Garden Birds* and many more titles (Collins)
Collins Gem Guides: everything from *Garden Birds* to *Wild Flowers* and much more (Collins)
The Natural History of Selborne, Gilbert White (many editions available)
Complete British Wildlife, Paul Sterry (Collins)
Fauna Britannica, Stefan Buczacki (Hamlyn)

Children's nature guides

All About Garden Wildlife, David Chandler (New Holland)
RSPB Children's Guide to Birdwatching, Chandler & Unwin (Helm)
My First Book of Garden Birds, Whittley & Unwin (A&C Black)
Nature Detectives' Handbook (Miles Kelly Publishing)
Usborne Spotter's Guide: Urban Wildlife (Usborne)
Town, Park & Garden Wildlife Discovery Pack (Green Bug Productions)
Nick Baker's Bug Book, Nick Baker (New Holland)

Wildlife in your garden

Attracting Birds to your Garden, Moss & Cottridge (New Holland)
The Garden Bird Handbook, Stephen Moss (New Holland)
The Secret Lives of Garden Birds, Dominic Couzens (Helm)
The Secret Lives of Garden Wildlife, Dominic Couzens (Helm)
Attracting Wildlife to your Garden, Burton & Tipling (New Holland)
How to Make a Wildlife Garden, Chris Baines (Frances Lincoln)
Guide to Garden Wildlife, Richard Lewington (British Wildlife)

Birds

RSPB Pocket Guide to the Birds of Britain, Harrap & Nurney (Helm)
RSPB Handbook of British Birds, Holden & Cleeves (Helm)
Collins Field Guide to Bird Songs and Calls, Geoff Sample (Collins)
The Secret Lives of Birds, Dominic Couzens (Helm)
Birds Britannica, Cocker & Mabey (Chatto & Windus)

Mammals

Collins Field Guide to the Mammals of Britain and Europe,
  Macdonald & Barrett (HarperCollins)
Complete British Animals, Paul Sterry (Collins)

Insects

Complete British Insects, Michael Chinery (Collins)
Britain's Butterflies, Tomlinson & Still (WildGuides)
Discover Butterflies in Britain, D.E. Newland (WildGuides)
Concise Guide to the Moths of Great Britain and Ireland,
  Townsend, Waring & Lewington (British Wildlife)
Enjoying Moths, Roy Leverton (Poyser)
Field Guide to the Dragonflies & Damselflies of Britain and Ireland,
  Brooks & Lewington (British Wildlife Publishing)

Wild Flowers & Trees

Field Guide to the Wild Flowers of Britain (Reader's Digest)
Wild Flowers of Britain & Ireland, Blamey, Fitter & Fitter (A&C Black)
The Wild Flower Key, Francis Rose (Warne)
Collins Tree Guide, Johnson & More (Collins)
Flora Britannica, Richard Mabey (Chatto & Windus)

Magazines

BBC Wildlife www.bbcwildlifemagazine.com
BBC Countryfile www.bbccountryfile.com
Birdwatch www.birdwatch.co.uk
Birdwatching www.birdwatching.co.uk

Acknowledgements

Many of my friends and colleagues have given their time, suggestions and advice during the writing of this book. They include Sarah Blunt, Dominic Couzens, Mike Dilger, Chris Ellis, Miranda Krestovnikoff, Rod Leslie, Rick Minter, Jeremy Mynott, Daniel Osorio, Bethan Smallwood, Stephen Ward and Brett Westwood.

I should also like to thank the staff of various conservation organisations who have been so supportive and enthusiastic. They include Jim Burt, Roger Key, Jonathan Pearce, Kate Russell, Guy Thompson and Julian Woolford at Natural England; Jill Attenborough and Graham Blight at the Woodland Trust; Matthew Oates, Sophie Gaffney, Mike Collins and Lucy Edwards at the National Trust; and Stephanie Hilborne, Jules Acton and Anna Guthrie at the Wildlife Trusts.

At Random House, my editor Rosemary Davidson has been a great support, and the book has benefitted hugely from her editorial skill and vision. I should also like to thank Simon Rhodes in the Production Department, and Louise Rhind-Tutt, Kay Peddle, Patrick Hargadon and Claire Morrison in the Random House Marketing and Publicity Department. The illustrators, David Atkinson, David Daly, Lizzie Harper, Nicole Heidirapour, Mike Langman and Chris Shields, and the designer, Friederike Huber.

My agent, Broo Doherty, deserves very special thanks. She encouraged me to develop an idea originally written as a feature for the *Guardian* into a book proposal; and was then perceptive enough to recognise that what was needed was not a book about the *problems* of Nature-deficit Disorder, but one offering real solutions.

Chris Baines has been an inspiration to me ever since we worked together on the BBC-TV series 'The Big E', way back in the 1980s. Chris has always been a prophet ahead of his time, and is at last being recognised for his visionary zeal in identifying so many vital environmental problems – and more importantly, devising ways to solve them. Chris spotted the issue of Nature

Deficit Disorder long before most people, and continues to inspire us all to help bring children back to nature.

This book is dedicated to David and Martine Osorio, parents of my dear friend Daniel. When I was a teenager the Osorios took me under their wing, allowing Daniel and me to explore wild places up and down the country. Without their guidance, and Daniel's friendship, I very much doubt if I would have continued my interest in the natural world. I hope that they, and their other children Rachel, Thomas and Jessica, will enjoy this book; and use it to encourage their own children and grandchildren to get closer to nature.

I must of course thank my family. My late mother, Kay Moss, and my late grandmother, Edna Vale, who despite constantly fearing for my safety, allowed their precious little boy to get his hands and knees dirty and explore nature. My late father, Franco Clerici, who sadly died while I was writing the book; my stepmother Angela and my dear sisters Elisabetta and Arianna. My older sons David and James, who continue to maintain an air of tolerant amusement regarding my passion for wildlife. And especially my younger children, Charlie, George and Daisy, who are learning to love nature at our home in Somerset. I am sure they will continue to enjoy birds, moths, butterflies and (especially) snails for the rest of their lives.

And finally, to my darling Suzanne, who has opened my eyes to what really matters in life, and who will always be there with me, watching and enjoying the wild world.

Stephen Moss
Mark, Somerset; December 2008.

Published by Square Peg
2 4 6 8 10 9 7 5 3 1

Copyright © Stephen Moss 2009

Colour illustrations © 2009 Lizzie Harper, except
© pp 236–7, 2009 David Atkinson; © pp 32–3, 46–7, 244–5, 2009 David Daly;
© pp 126–7, 2009 Mike Langman; © pp 140–1, Chris Shields
Black and white illustrations © 2009 Nicole Heidaripour
Designed by Friederike Huber

First published in Great Britain in 2009 by
Square Peg
Random House, 20 Vauxhall Bridge Road,
London SW1V 2SA
www.rbooks.co.uk

Addresses for companies within The Random House Group Limited can be found at:
www.randomhouse.co.uk/offices.htm

The Random House Group Limited Reg. No. 954009

A CIP catalogue record for this book
is available from the British Library

ISBN 9780224086165

The Random House Group Limited makes every effort to ensure that the papers used in its books are
made from trees that have been legally sourced from well-managed and credibly certified forests. Our
paper procurement policy can be found at: www.randomhouse.co.uk/paper.htm

Printed and bound in China by
C&C Offset Printing Co.